Living with Confidence

Living a blessed life with meaning can only function when you trust in something bigger than yourself – Trust God.

One advantage in trusting God is a life of serenity, even during challenging times, like soaring across the sky in an aircraft, knowing God is the pilot.

Elena N. Sifuentes

Life's Journey – Living for God
Copyright @ 2021 by Elena N. Sifuentes

All Rights Reserved. No portion of this book may be reproduced, stored in a retrieval system, or transmitted in any form or by any means - electronic, mechanical, photocopy, recording, scanning, or other - except for brief quotations in critical reviews or articles, without the prior written permission of the publisher. Subject to permission under action 107 and/or 108 of the 1976 United States Copyright act. Request for permission should be addressed to the publisher at elenasifuent919@gmail.com.

First paperback edition August 2021

ISBN 978-1-7351400-4-9 (paperback)
ISBN 978-1-7351400-5-6 (eBook)

Published by Elena N. Sifuentes

Please note: Every effort has been made to ensure the accuracy of the information throughout this book. The information is believed to be accurate at the time of printing. The publisher and author are not responsible for errors or omissions for changes to details or the consequences of the reader's reliance on the information provided.

Readers are welcome to contact the publisher for comments, updates, or questions at elenasifuentes919@gmail.com.

Contents

Dedication 7

Acknowledgment 9

Introduction... 11

Chapter 1   Choosing the Right Path 15

Chapter 2   The Narrow Gate and Road 21

Chapter 3   Rags to Riches............................... 30
    A Case Study on Queen Esther................ 31
    A Case Study on Tyler Perry 36
    A Case Study on Do Won Chang 40
    A Case Study on Jesus Christ.................... 44
        Born in a Stable 48
        Magi – Wise Men 52
        Homeless?... 55
        No Place to Lay.................................. 57
        Borrowed 60
            Jesus Borrowed a
            Donkey, a Colt, the Foal
            of a Donkey 60
            Jesus Borrows Boats................... 63

  Jesus Buried in a
   Borrowed Tomb 65
 Taxes 68
 Crucified but not Dead 71

Chapter 4 God Uses the Weak 78

Chapter 5 Redemption 105
  Mephibosheth 105
  Cornealious Anderson 108
  The Prodigal Son 111

Chapter 6 Walking in Someone Else's Shoes ... 114
 King David 115
 I. David's accomplishments 117
  God anointed David 117
  David's Allegiance to God 119
  David Defeated Goliath 120
  David the Lyrist 124
  David the Psalmist 125
  David Conquered Jerusalem 129
  The Ark of the Covenant 131
  Ministering before the Ark of
  the Lord 134
  God's covenant with David 135
   While David was alive 136
   Promises Made after
   David Dies 136
  David's Confidence Was in
  God, not with Self 138

II.	List of Some of David's Failures. 139
	Adultery and Murder 140
	David's Son's Demise 143
	Unauthorized Census and a Plague.... 144
	David's Life Summary...................... 147

    Jerry Givens... 149
    Eric Liddell.. 153
    Bethany Hamilton.................................... 155

Chapter 7   From Atheism to Christianity 159
    C.S. Lewis 161
    John Gilmour 164
    Phil Hemsley.. 167

Chapter 8   God Uses Ordinary People........... 169
    Chuck Norris 169
    Corrie ten Boom 173

Chapter 9   Transformation 178

Chapter 10 Conclusion................................... 185

About the Author... 189

Dedication

I dedicate this book to God Almighty, who has inspirited me to be a writer. Through the leading of the Holy Spirit and the confidence I have in Jesus Christ, I am able to accomplish such a task as this. My trust is in God and God alone. He is my tower of strength as He protects all who run to Him.

> Jehovah is my rock, and my
> fortress, and my deliverer;
> My God, my rock, in whom I will take refuge;
> My shield, and the horn of my
> salvation, my high tower.
> Psalm 18:2 ASV

Acknowledgment

Throughout this journey as a writer, my niece, Catherine Olen, has been a tremendous asset through both her guidance and expertise in writing books and publishing. Catherine is an entrepreneur and author of several books about the lives and deaths of Hollywood celebrities and theme park travel guides.

Thanks to Ben L Wells, III and Angeleena Wells, for their continued encouragement throughout this process.

Introduction

Life's journey is met with many highs and downward spirals, creating challenges or hurtle depending on how we react to them. God does not promise a life well-manicured; the fall of Adam and Eve threw that idea out the window. However, he promises never to forsake us or leave us stranded in the miry clay or slimy pit of destruction. Instead, he gives us a firm foundation to stand upon (see Psalm 40:2). God has the power to help the weak and the grace to help the undeserving if we choose to put our trust in Him. Life is a transformation from a sinful human nature, a life seeking fleshly gratification, into a divine nature, a life filled with the fruit of the Spirit. "The fruit of the Spirit is love, joy, peace, forbearance, kindness, goodness, faithfulness, gentleness, and self-control" Galatians 5:22-23 NIV.

> *He lifted me out of the slimy pit, out of the mud and mire; he set my feet on a rock and gave me a firm place to stand.*
> *Psalm 40:2 NIV*

In life's journey, we can choose various roads, which are often influenced by our upbringing. Some paths lead us astray in which we need to stop, think, reevaluate, and ask ourselves, "At the end of our life's journey, will we end up where we want to be, or perhaps is this road a distraction and the long way in accomplishing our goal?" We don't want to be like the Israelites, who took 40 years to arrive in the promised land of Canaan when it should have taken only 11 days (Deuteronomy 1:2). Wandering in the wilderness was the result of their disobedience and unbelief in God's word and promises. We don't want to take the wrong road, leading to many regrets or, worse, eternal damnation.

> *It is eleven days' journey from Horeb by the way of Mount Seir to Kadesh-Barnea.*
> *Deuteronomy 1:2 ESV*

In this book, we will take a look at how people throughout history handled times of adversity. While seeking God's direction amidst challenging times, many experienced God's mercy and grace, second chances, redemption, and altogether life transformation. Before we get into all that, let me tell you a story about when I strayed off the right trail.

While on vacation with my family members, we ventured onto a beautiful trail in Sedona, Arizona.

I had gotten to a point where I felt I should go back before I got too tired, so I left the group and headed to the parking lot. Even though I knew the path I needed to take to get back, somehow, I found myself at a higher altitude and on the wrong path (the height allowed a breath-taking, beautiful, panoramic view reflecting the glory of God's hand). The first inclination that I was not on the right path was when I realized that nothing around me looked familiar. I stopped and said, "Oh Lord, what did I do, and how am I going to find my way to the parking lot?" I decided to go back down to where I started climbing. I turned around and began descending, and once at the bottom of the hill, I saw a sign with arrows pointing towards the path to the parking lot. Once I started back on the right path, I stopped to speak with a few bicyclists, and to my surprise, the group that I left behind passed alongside me and ahead of me.

Chapter 1

Choosing the Right Path

When thinking about your life's journey, your past, where you are now, and where you hope to be in the future, consider setting goals. I like to use the saying, "Life without goals leads to a boring and unproductive life." Goals provide direction, and without goals, there are no finish lines nor any meaningful purpose for living life. The dangers of not following a plan can lead us to emptiness and a life filled with regrets, drifting aimlessly and being tossed around by the storms of life. We often end up searching for the meaning of life in all the wrong places.

While making choices for our lives, we can make more than one choice or take more than one path. God's desire for us is to live in righteousness, to have a meaningful life filled with gratification, contentment, and peace even during times of conflict, trials, tribulation, and disappointment. On the other hand, choices can result in a lifetime of disappointments, chasing after what can never please or exchanging true peace for worldly success: wealth, fame, and/or power. We have seen famous celebrities that appeared to be happy or on top of the world, accomplishing goals most of us will never see in our lifetime. Yet, they were disillusioned by the promise of grandeur and ended up committing suicide. People that have won mega millions from the Lottery, sweepstakes, or perhaps have been handed large sums of money through inheritance have gone from riches to rags. Lacking wisdom and self-control, many formerly wealthy individuals have ended up in bankruptcy because they have mismanaged their money, failed to acquire good business skills, and/or spent it all living a lavish lifestyle. There is only one true way to a fulfilled life: igniting our hearts with a passion for following God. Living a righteous life, trusting God by focusing on what pleases Him, and accepting Jesus Christ as our Savior and Lord is the only way to be truly fulfilled. On this road, God will direct our path, and all our accomplishments will come with a blessing, and we will be filled with God's peace.

Our motivation can stem from either a selfish ambition or from a servant's heart of love. To live a life pleasing to God, we need to follow Jesus' example as He not only spoke of what was needed, but

He demonstrated throughout his journey on earth the path we should take. Throughout Jesus' life, he demonstrated servanthood, He preached the good news (the Gospel which is available to all of us), He delivered people by casting out demons (freeing people from the influence of evil spirits), and He physically healed many. Also, Jesus kept in communication with God the Father through prayer, thus demonstrating His love for Him. God seeks a personal relationship with His children, and it pleases God when we seek after the kingdom of God.

You may ask, "What does it mean to have a personal relationship with God?" A personal relationship begins when we realize we need God. In a time when I was at my lowest, I was hopeless and knew I needed help. Then, while at church, when an altar call was announced that I went forward and said, "Since my way is not working, I'll try God's way." I asked God to forgive me with a repentful heart and accepted Jesus Christ as my Savior and Lord. The journey does not end there, though. God desires to have a close relationship like you would with any other loved one. When you get up in the morning, what is the first thing you do? You say good morning to your loved ones. That's exactly what God desires. He wants an intimate relationship. He wants us to communicate with Him every day. Communication can first start with a prayer, greeting the Lord, praising Him, worshiping Him, and requesting His help for our needs and those of our family and friends. God also communicates through the reading of His Word, the Bible, and meditating on what we have read as the Lord reveals His message to us. One of the most important prayer requests should be to ask God for wisdom (James 1:5, 3:17), as God's wisdom leads to a peaceful life.

> *If any of you lacks wisdom, you should ask God, who gives generously to all without finding fault, and it will be given to you.*
> *James 1:5 NIV*

> *But the wisdom that comes from heaven is first of all pure; then peace-loving, considerate, submissive, full of mercy and good fruit, impartial and sincere.*
> *James 3:17 NIV*

Throughout the Bible, there are guidelines for living a Christian life. Proverbs is a good resource and a place to understand what pleases God and brings us fulfillment. Let's look at Proverbs 15:33 and Proverbs 9:10-12, for example. These two proverbs tell us we are to reverently fear the Lord because it is the beginning of wisdom. Furthermore, wisdom teaches us to live a righteous life, that is, to refrain from sin, trust and obey God, respect the law of the land, and choose to serve God rather than ourselves. Wisdom also instructs us that humility comes before honor and the opposite of humility is pride. Pride seeks to obtain and fulfill whatever promotes self-pleasure. Biblical humility is something that we cannot obtain without the Spirit of God working in our lives. We are not born with humility, as we all want to be given recognition, honor, and affirmation for jobs well done. We naturally seek what benefits us before others, and we are concerned with our image rather than that of Christ. We see through Jesus' example that wisdom and humility work together.

First, Christ humbled Himself when He relinquished all the privileges He shared with God when He became a man and a servant.

Second, He was humiliated through the crucifixion by dying a criminal's death on the cross.

Third, He was brought to a place of honor, seated at the right hand of God. With humility, we too can acknowledge that God's way, following His will, is better than our way. Our reliance on Him pleases Him. Following the guidelines of these verses not only assures us wisdom when we reverently fear the Lord, but it also promises a long life. However, if we are a mocker, we alone will suffer the consequences of our heedless decisions.

> *Wisdom's instruction is to fear the LORD, and humility comes before honor.*
> *Proverbs 15:33 NIV*

> *The fear of the LORD is the beginning of wisdom, and knowledge of the Holy One is understanding. For through wisdom your days will be many, and years will be added to your life. If you are wise, your wisdom will reward you; if you are a mocker, you alone will suffer.*
> *Proverbs 9:10-12 NIV*

The journey of life is composed of daily choices determined by the paths we choose to take every time we make a decision. Choosing wisdom will bring blessings, while rejecting wisdom will bring punishment. Remember the adage; what you sow, you will reap. Good behavior is taught from the moment we are born. Toddlers are taught not to touch the fire, or they will get burned. Teenagers cannot get a license to drive unless they have passed the required driving exams. Similarly, we need to learn the truths recorded in the Bible to understand what is needed to live a life pleasing to God.

Chapter 2

The Narrow Gate and Road

Which road will you take? Jesus often spoke in parables, and when Jesus gave His Sermon on the Mount, He spoke about the choice between the small gate and narrow road versus the wide gate and broad road. Two ways to live, and yet only one leads to eternal (spiritual) life. The road we need to take to ensure that we accomplish our goal as a Christian is to enter through the narrow gate and road that leads to life (Matthew 7:13-14). The two different gates represent two different kingdoms. The first is the kingdom of the world, also referred to as the path of the wicked, which leads to destruction and eternal ruin. The other gate is the kingdom of heaven, which leads to the path of righteousness and eternal life and blessings.

> *Enter through the narrow gate.*
> *For wide is the gate and broad is*
> *the road that leads to destruction,*

> *and many enter through it. But small is the gate and narrow the road that leads to life, and only a few find it.*
> *Matthew 7:13-14 NIV*

As a Christian, true discipleship requires that once justified by grace, we honor and glorify the Lord through the acceptance of Jesus Christ as our personal savior. In this passage, Matthew 7:13-14, there are two messages the writer wants to convey.

- First, the 'road' symbolizes the path to either heaven or hell.
    - a) The narrow road is the difficult path in which we can only enter through faith (the acceptance of Jesus Christ, the only mediator to the Father) by the grace of God.
    - b) The broad road is the path that many will take because it is the easy way. You do not have to choose this path; you are already on it, leading to eternal destruction.

- The second message is instruction Jesus gives His disciples for their spiritual journey in contrast with life on the path devoid of God.

a) The spiritual life is a blessed life in which we glorify the Lord. It often requires making difficult choices or engaging in difficult tasks while following the Lord's will.
b) For a Christian who has fallen off the path, life ends up being unfruitful and can lead to a destructive lifestyle that does not honor the Lord.

The narrow gate/road (the entrance or pathway to eternal life) refers to a path that requires effort and intentional focus by keeping our eyes on the goal, the Kingdom of God. It is a difficult road, especially when challenges come from non-believers, who may look down on followers of Christ when persecution occurs. Jesus said He was the door, and all must enter through Him (John 10:9). It is a new spiritual birth given by the grace of God in Jesus Christ. It requires a commitment to be disciplined, honoring the Lord by surrendering our will to God's will and accepting the challenges that will come. Some may be easy, some may be hard, but they are always rewarding. Jesus said that we must bear our cross and seek after Him to be one of His disciples (Luke 14:27). In Roman times, carrying a cross inevitably meant death, as one would only carry a cross to the site of their own hanging. Ultimately, our goal is to love the Lord with all our hearts, souls, and minds and stand strong, following the Lord's commandments with all our hearts.

> *I am the gate; whoever enters through me will be saved. They will come in and go out, and find pasture.*
>
> *John 10:9 NIV*
>
> *And whoever does not carry their cross and follow me cannot be my disciple.*
>
> *Luke 14:27 NIV*

Following God's will means we are to strive to live in righteousness by meditating on the Word of God and following the instructions recorded in the Bible. Also, our commitment should include serving others and putting them first to the point that we are willing to surrender our life for a brother. Jesus instructs us to love our enemies and bless those that curse us (Matthew 5:44). At times, this can seem difficult, seemingly one that we cannot accomplish, but with God, all things are possible. This verse expands Jesus' teaching to love our neighbor, not take revenge, and pray for those who persecute us. When we pray for our enemy, we are not harboring resentment towards our enemy, which can hinder our health. In addition, we are to repent and confess our sins to one another. But most importantly, all of us must make a deliberate decision to accept the gift of God to enter the narrow gate. We are to acknowledge that we are sinners and that we are saved through faith when we accept Jesus Christ as our Savior and Lord, we are saved (Ephesians 2:8-9).

> *But I tell you, love your enemies and pray for those who persecute you,*
>
> *For it is by grace you have been saved, through faith —and this is not from yourselves, it is the gift of God— not by works, so that no one can boast.*
> *Ephesians 2:8-9 NIV*

Billy Graham says the broad road is "Lacking in faith, convictions, morals, and obedience to God."[1] The path of least resistance does not require us to make a decision. In fact, it leads us on a destructive path, which is referred to as eternal ruin, where diversity of lifestyles, philosophies and the ungodly living exist. It leads to the seemingly attractive things of the world that tempt us and habits that go against the Word of God, which is met with constant ruin. A life without God's help can end up in despera-

---

[1] https://www.arcamax.com/healthandspirit/religion/billygraham/s-2250706

tion and magnifies the pain, depression, and hurts of this world, ultimately separating us from God if we do not repent. Some examples of an ungodly life are: not loving the Lord your God with all your heart, soul, and mind, not loving your neighbor as yourself, worshipping other gods, taking the name of God in vain, not keeping the Sabbath day holy, not honoring our father and mother, murdering, committing adultery, stealing, bearing false witness against our neighbor and coveting. Additionally, we are to reframe from such things as lust, rage, slander, pride, jealousy, and filthy language.

Since everyone wants to be accepted and be a part of the crowd, it is difficult to turn away from rebellious, ungodly friends or family to follow the narrow road of obedience. In Matthew 10:37-38, Jesus emphasizes the importance of choosing Him above all others, including our family. We are to rely on the Lord for His promises to help us in time of need, as He is only a prayer away.

> *Anyone who loves their father or mother more than me is not worthy of me; anyone who loves their son or daughter more than me is not worthy of me. Whoever does not take up their cross and follow me is not worthy of me.*
> *Matthew 10:37-38 NIV*

We must also beware that we are not misled by false prophets, who put on a show of faith, fooling us into thinking they are God's messengers. Some people believe that the wide gate and the broad way lead to heaven, but that is not what Jesus was saying. In Matthew 7:15, Jesus warns us to be alert to false prophets, people that are clothed like sheep but inwardly are ferocious wolves. Sadly, some false prophets and their followers may truly believe in what they are teaching, but in reality, their beliefs oppose the Word of God and, more importantly, show that they are not following the will of God. Jesus said we must do the will of God (Matthew 7:21). The will of God acknowledges that God's plan is His sovereign and supreme will. The control of everything is in His hands, even evil deeds. Let's look at Herod, Pilot, the soldiers, and the Jewish leaders God used to fulfill his plan as he allowed them to Crucify Jesus (Isaiah 53:10). Jesus referred to God as His Father as He was fulfilling the will of God through the crucifixion. Even though God hates evil deeds, He allows events to take place for our good and to accomplish His sovereign will. God's will commands us to be thankful, knowing that He is our provider, healer, protector, deliverer and that He is the I AM (He is available for whatever needs we have). In 1Thessalonians 4:3, the will of God is defined as living in holiness, sanctified, and refraining from sexual immorality. Also, in Matthew 7:21, we are reminded that not everyone that calls on the Lord will enter the kingdom of heaven, only those that do the will of the Father. The will of God is to enter the gate by following the gospel of Jesus Christ with genuine faith and humility. In John 14:6, Jesus referred to Himself as 'the way, the truth, and the life and no one goes to the Father except through Jesus.'

> *"Watch out for false prophets. They come to you in sheep's clothing, but inwardly they are ferocious wolves.*
> Matthew 7:15 NIV

> *Many will say to me on that day, 'Lord, Lord, did we not prophesy in your name and in your name drive out demons and, in your name, perform many miracles?' Then I will tell them plainly, 'I never knew you. Away from me, you evildoers!'*
> Matthew 7:22-23 NIV

> *"Not everyone who says to me, 'Lord, Lord,' will enter the kingdom of heaven, but only the one who does the will of my Father who is in heaven.*
> Matthew 7:21 NIV

*Yet it was the LORD's will to crush him and cause him to suffer, and though the LORD makes his life an offering for sin,
he will see his offspring and prolong his days,
and the will of the LORD will prosper in his hand.*
>> Isaiah 53:10 NIV

It is God's will that you should be sanctified: that you should avoid sexual immorality.
>> 1 Thessalonians 4:3 NIV

Jesus answered, "I am the way and the truth and the life. No one comes to the Father except through me.
>> John 14:6 NIV

Chapter 3

Rags to Riches

We celebrate when the underdog wins or someone overcomes unforeseen challenges. After a Hallmark-type move, I always say, "And they lived happily ever after." Life is filled with many stories that have distinctive characteristics, filled with unforeseen challenges. We need to pray to God for help in these situations, that His will be done, and that we keep the faith and don't give up. Positive thinking and especially keeping our eyes on God's plan for our lives enable us to rise above these challenges. That's why we should focus on the many stories that can encourage us not to give up, be patient, and trust God.

Everyone has a past. Some are filled with contentment and familial support. Others are defined by poverty and a lack of parental involvement, but in every case, as life has enfolded, the disappointments, joys, and challenges we have faced have shaped and molded us. Our past, however, does not have to dictate what our future will look like. There are many examples of people in the Bible and throughout history that either fell on hard times or grew up in poverty but rose to the challenge and succeeded. These people did not allow their past to control their future but instead were determined to improve their life's circumstances. Some people acknowledge the mercy and grace God provided to help them overcome hardship and are thankful for the opportunity to accept and follow His ways.

- A Case Study on Queen Esther:

The Book of Esther, found in the Old Testament, contains a good example of someone (Queen Esther) who went from rags to riches yet remained faithful to God. Esther is a Persian name that means "star," and her Hebrew name was Hadassah. She was exceptionally beautiful, as she had a beautiful figure and face. She was also an orphan because she lost both her parents and an older cousin, by the name of Mordecai, raised her like his own daughter. Esther lived in exile, like many Jewish people scattered throughout Persia after the Babylonian exile. The Jewish people did not want to return to Jerusalem because it was in a war-torn state. Can you imagine losing both your parents and being far away from your home? This had to be a scary time for her. In times like this, God steps in to protect us and care for us. I have to admit that sometimes it's not what we hoped for, but God uses all circumstances to accomplish His eternal goals. In the end, He is always right as He knows the future and exactly what we need.

In this story, we are introduced to the Persian King Xerxes, also known as Ahasuerus, known for his lavish banquets, excessive drinking, jarring temper, and sexual appetite. Does this describe anyone you may know? One day, the king was angry at his wife, Vashti, because she refused to go to him when he ordered her to do so. Having had too much wine during a seven-day drunken celebration, the king wanted Vashti to wear her royal crown and parade in front of the guests so that he could display her beauty to the people. Knowing that the king was intoxicated, she refused to be exploited; thus, she disobeyed his demand. When you disobey a king, you know what's coming next, consequences! The king banished Vashti and ordered a nationwide beauty pageant so that he could replace her with another beautiful queen. The decree was made, and the king's edict commenced searching for a beautiful young virgin for the King. Now Esther was taken captive against her will during this search, along with all the other young women. All of the ladies were taken to the citadel of Susa. Hegai, the king's eunuch, was put in charge of preparing the harem so that they could meet the King. Esther pleased Hegai and won his favor, so he gave her special attention. While waiting with all the other women, Mordecai gave Esther strict orders not to reveal her nationality and family background because the Persians hated Jews, and Mordecai was unsure what the outcome would be if she revealed this information.

Before the women appeared before the King, they completed twelve months of beauty treatments and were allowed to take anything they chose from the harem to the king's palace. When Esther's turn came up, she would only take what Hegai suggested. She was taken to King Xerxes, and the king was attracted to her and won his favor above all the other women. Thus, the king set a royal crown on her head and made her queen, replacing Vashti. We can say she went from rags to riches, but her story does not end there. Let's continue and see how God used an obedient young lady to accomplish his goal of not allowing the Jewish people to be annihilated.

Meanwhile, Mordecai uncovered a conspiracy to assassinate King Xerxes. He told Queen Esther, who reported it to the king, giving credit to Mordecai. Haman, the king's second in command, hated the Jews. He was greatly feared, and all the royal officials at the king's gate knelt and paid honor to Haman as the king commanded. But Mordecai did not kneel, nor did he honor him. When Haman found out that Mordecai refused to bow down, he was enraged. Seeing that Mordecai was a Jew, he wanted to kill Mordecai and all the Jews throughout King Xerxes's kingdom. Haman convinced King Xerxes to kill all the Jews because he said that they not only opposed the king, but they did not obey his laws. When Mordecai learned about this plot to kill all the Jews, he persuaded Esther to help by going in to see the king and beg for mercy. She had to plead with him to save her people.

Mordecai, the Jewish people, and Esther had fasted and prayed before her going to see the king not only for favor but because it was against the king's rule to enter uninvited. At the risk of execution, she courageously entered the inner court of the palace. The king was sitting on his royal throne in the hall facing the entrance when he saw her. Supposing that she had something important to ask of him, he allowed her to enter and assured her that she would not die. To show that he was pleased with her, he held out the gold scepter indicating that she was to enter. Her request was to invite the king and Haman to a banquet she prepared later that day. At the banquet, the king asked Esther regarding her petition, and he promised it would be given. Esther asked that her life would be spared, along with her people. She explained to the king that Haman had plotted for her people to be destroyed, killed, and annihilated. The king was disturbed because he remembered how Mordecai, a Jew, had exposed the plot to assassinate him. The king decided to reward Mordecai for his good deed and ordered Haman to be impaled on a pole reaching a height of fifty cubits (75 feet). This was the very pole Haman had prepared for Mordecai as punishment for refusing to bow down to him. Once again, Esther pleaded with the king to put an end to the evil plan of Haman. The king wrote another decree on behalf of the Jews. Thus, God's plan to save the Jews from the hands of Haman was complete.

This example shows that Esther was a poor orphan girl who obeyed her older cousin Mordecai. God knew He would trust her, so He used her to save her life and that of the Jewish race from the hand of an evil Haman. Her God-given beauty brought favor from many people, especially King Xerxes, who took her to be his queen. This is an example of someone who showed humility, was obedient and was brought to a place of honor.

You may say, 'the story of Esther is an old Bible story told centuries ago; show me a modern-day rag to riches story where God is front and center.' The story of Tyler Perry, a Christian, an American actor, writer, film producer/playwright, and director, is one of my favorites.

- **A Case Study on Tyler Perry:**

Emmitt Perry Jr. changed his name to Tyler Perry to distance himself from his dad, Emmitt Perry Sr. Tyler was born and raised in New Orleans in poverty and in an abusive home. Tyler had a tough childhood. His dad abused not only Tyler but also his mom, Willie Maxine Perry. He and his mom met with regular beatings, shouting matches, and lots of name-callings. Tyler was physically and sexually abused at home and molested by others outside of the family.

Unlike his dad, Tyler's mom was not abusive, taking Tyler to church each week. Tyler felt that church was a safe haven, and he found contentment in God. Tyle said in an interview that he got through these difficult times by turning to God and forgiving his tormentors. To cope with the abuse at home, he would imagine himself running and playing in a park. At one point, his mother was so fed up with the abuse, she packed the children into the car and drove to California. Unfortunately, his dad reported the vehicle stolen, and they were put in jail until his dad went to get them. The dad drove them back to Louisiana, beating his mother all the way home. After enduring another vicious beating by his dad, Tyler finally ran away to live with his Aunt Jerry, who kept watch over him and protected him.

While he was a young boy, Tyler wrote down his thoughts and experiences in the form of a letter to himself, and this was the dream and inspiration for the beginnings of his career in which the Lord inspired him to write his first play. In the play, Tyler created himself as he played the character of Madea, a tough elderly lady. Willie was the inspiration for this famous character. Tyler had hoped to present the opening of his play to a packed audience, but every seat was empty. For several years, Tyler invested the remainder of his savings on new shows, but each one was a flop, and he began to run out of money. Even while working odd jobs, he continued to run out of money and found himself living on the streets, in his car, or at homeless shelters. It took approximately six years before that first play would finally be a sellout, forcing the production to be moved to a bigger venue, the Fox Theatre in Atlanta. Tyler has since created various films, live stage plays (many of the stage plays were adopted as films), and television series. In addition, as an actor, he has been in films that he did not direct nor produce. His career also includes writing books, which have sold thousands of copies and earning titles like The New York Times Best Seller, Book of the Year, and Best Humor Book at the Quill Awards.

As Tyler became more successful, he acquired the former army base, Fort McPherson (330-acre), located in the heart of Atlanta, converting it into a major movie studio and production facility. It is currently registered on the National Registry for Historic Places. Tyler Perry Studio is one of the largest film studios in the nation with forty buildings, including twelve state-of-the-art sound stages. In addition, the facilities include back lots, a baseball field, retail shops, a jail, a trailer park, a mansion, a duplicate of the White House, and other historic buildings. This established Tyler Perry as the first African-American to outright own a major film studio.[2]

This story should be an encouragement to all of us. No matter what our past has thrown our way, like Tyler, who endured a tremendous share of disappointments, with patience, hard work, perseverance, faith, guidance, and trust in God, there is always hope.

When making life decisions, we must search our hearts to see where God is leading us. Not everyone is born with a silver spoon in their mouth, where doors seem to open, and life opportunities come easily, but everyone can take the challenges of life and use them for good. There's a saying I have heard, "The lower they fall, the higher they rise."

---

[2] https://www.nytimes.com/2019/10/02/movies/tyler-perry-atlanta.html

Starting from the bottom does not have to be bad because there is only one way to go, and that is up.

In Jeremiah 29:11, the prophet Jeremiah said that in the challenges of life, in the longevity of suffering and hardship, we can take comfort knowing that God will eventually rescue us. Though it may not be an immediate answer to prayer, our best growth comes through persevering. God has a plan for our lives and a promise that He will carry us through to the end to prosper us, not harm us, but to give us hope and a future. We are instructed to trust God and not give up as difficulties such as the pandemic, loss of income, or family confront us, for God's plan for good is unfolding.

God's plans are different than ours. He sees the entire picture from an eternal perspective; after all, He is omniscient; that is, He knows everything, the past, present, and the future. In Tyler Perry's case, God did not answer his prayer immediately. Actually, it took years of failure, dreams unfulfilled, and difficult days before God's blessings came about. God will stretch our faith to take us into a closer walk with Him as we learn to put our faith and trust in His timing. Psalm 37:7 reminds us to take great comfort when overwhelmed with current events in our life. We are to wait upon the Lord, to rest in Him, and be patient. By faith, we can be confident in the power and promises of God.

> *For I know the plans I have for you," declares the LORD, "plans to prosper you and not to harm you, plans to give you hope and a future.*
>
> Jeremiah 29:11 NIV

> *Be still before the LORD and wait patiently for him; do not fret when people succeed in their ways, when they carry out their wicked schemes.*
>
> Psalm 37:7 NIV

• A Case Study on Do Won Chang:

Do Won Chang is an amazing story of an immigrant from Seoul, South Korea. Born in a village called Myron-Dong, Do Won's life is one of faith, perseverance, and flexibility. His success story is a testament to the faithfulness of God and Do Won's unwavering faith.

Do Won Chang's nickname is Don. He grew up working in coffee shops, eventually starting his own coffee delivery service in South Korea. He was "an entrepreneur in the making." He and his wife Jin Sook Chang moved to America in the early 1980s with the idea of starting a business. With a good ethical mindset, he worked at three jobs: as a janitor, gas station attendant, and in a coffee shop. The avenue that caught his entrepreneurial eye was the fashion industry, in which he observed that wealthy people gravitated and worked in fashion. Back in those days, working people were required to follow a dress protocol, namely 'business attire.' The men wore suits and ties, no blue jeans, while women wore suits, heels, and nylons (later suit pants).

Wise money management allowed him to save and open his first retail store, *Fashion 21*, in Highland Park, a city in Los Angeles County, California. This first store was set to primarily target the Korean-American clientele. The first year was so successful that he changed the name to Forever 21, allowing him to expand the business by targeting more people in different areas of the United States and his hometown in South Korea. Presently he has stores throughout the world.

Don's commitment to God is demonstrated in his devotion to prayer, reading the Bible, and attending church. Furthermore, John 3:16 is printed on each of the carrier bags at all his stores; as a successful entrepreneur, he and his wife are generous philanthropists, donating money and time to various causes.

> *For God so loved the world that he gave his one and only Son, that whoever believes in him shall not perish but have eternal life.*
> *John 3:16 NIV*

Some of the causes the foundation supports, according to Erply.com, include:

> *Do Won Chang and Jin Sook run the Fashion Delivers Charitable Foundation, donating money to churches and other faith groups? They carry out missionary work in third-world countries.*
>
> *American Forest – planting trees from the sales of Forever 21's eco-totes*
>
> *Shoes That Fit – supporting underprivileged children in Los Angeles*
>
> *Haiti Earthquake Appeals – Forever 21 has donated over $5 million of clothing to those affected by the earthquake in Haiti*

> *Missing Persons' Foundation-Missing Person's has created national and international awareness for the causes and prevention of child abductions*
>
> *Starlight Foundation – helping seriously ill children. Forever 21 recruited celebrities including Demi Lovato and the Hilton sisters to design clothes for Forever 21's recent Starlight Campaign Chang has said that his mission in life is to help others, and the selling of clothes is his "tool" for doing that.*[3]

This story is such an encouragement for all of us to trust in God through Jesus Christ and to put into action the hard work of perseverance in faith, as God brings the visions and dreams he has given us to fruition. Chang's strong moral ethic and allegiance to God not only gave him the strength and fortitude to work consistently towards his goal, but God was able to use him for His glory while at the same time blessing him.

---

[3] https://erply.com/do-won-chang-is-best-known-for-founding-the-clothing-retail-store-forever-21/

• A Case Study on Jesus Christ:

The most spectacular success story known worldwide of someone going from rags to riches is that of Jesus Christ, my Lord. But I like to say that He went from riches to rags and then back to riches. The Bible describes heaven as a home with many spectacular mansions and streets of pure gold (Revelations 21:21). Yes, Jesus lived in splendor, in glory, while in Heaven, with unrestrained power and authority. Yet, the creator of the universe stepped down from His throne, setting aside his privileges. He came to earth as a human being, like you and me. Philippians 2:7 says that "Jesus emptied Himself by taking the form of a servant, being born in the likeness of man." In Philippians 2:6-8, we read that "even though He was the very nature of God, He did not consider equality with God, rather, He made Himself nothing by taking the very nature of a servant, being made in human likeness. he humbled himself by becoming obedient to death — even death on a cross."

> *Rather, he made himself nothing by taking the very nature of a servant, being made in human likeness.*
>
> *Philippians 2:7 NIV*

> *Who, being in very nature God, did not consider equality with God something to be used to his own advantage; rather, he made himself nothing by taking the very nature of a servant, being made in human likeness. And being found in appearance as a man, he humbled himself by becoming obedient to death—even death on a cross!*
> *Philippians 2:6-8 NIV*

The question of whether Jesus was 'poor' has been tossed around quite a bit. I have heard people say that He was poor based on the following reasons:

- He was born in a stable; this claim was taken from Luke 2:12, which states, *"This will be a sign to you: You will find a baby wrapped in cloths and lying in a manger."*
- Mary and Joseph did not offer a lamb but a poor man's offering when Jesus was presented to the Lord in the Temple. This was done during the time of purification for Mary (Luke 2:22), where a pair of turtledoves or two young pigeons were to be offered if one could not offer a lamb.
- Jesus didn't have a place to lay His head. This idea comes from Luke 9:58, which states that Jesus replied, *"Foxes have dens*

- Jesus had to borrow a boat as stated in Luke 5:3, *"He got into one of the boats, the one belonging to Simon, and asked him to put out a little from shore. Then he sat down and taught the people from the boat."*
- The colt that Jesus rode on when He entered Jerusalem was borrowed according to Matthew 21:2 when Jesus instructed the Disciples to *"Go to the village ahead of you, and at once you will find a donkey tied there, with her colt by her. Untie them and bring them to me. If anyone says anything to you, say that the Lord needs them, and he will send them right away."*
- The tomb in which His body was laid was borrowed. Luke 27:57-60 states, *"As evening approached, there came a rich man from Arimathea, named Joseph, who had himself become a disciple of Jesus. Going to Pilate, he asked for Jesus' body, and Pilate ordered that it be given to him. Joseph took the body, wrapped it in a clean linen cloth, and placed it in his own new tomb that he had cut out of the rock"*.

and birds have nests, but the Son of Man has no place to lay his head."

In 1 Corinthians 8:9, Paul urged the Corinthians to keep their commitment to give money to help Christians suffering from hardships. Paul also stated that while Jesus was rich in heaven, He chose to become poor by coming to earth, living in a world of suffering and death for our sakes, so that one day we could become rich.

> *For you know the grace of our Lord Jesus Christ, that though he was rich, yet for your sake he became poor, so that you through his poverty might become rich.*
> *1 Corinthians 8:9 NIV*

Let us explore the topic of Jesus' poverty further. Being 'Poor' has many meanings depending on one's circumstances. A rich man may say he is poor because he only has one Lamborghini, and his neighbor may have three. Yet, someone with very little may say they are rich because they have a place to call home, whether it is a shelter, small apartment, or in someone's garage. I say if you have shelter, clothing, food, and health, then you are rich.

Born in a Stable

The story of Jesus' birth in a stable has been passed down from generation to generation. Coming down to earth showed humility because Jesus gave up a majestic life for our sake. He was born in a stable in Bethlehem versus the comfort of a palace. In a time when the weather was frightful, the stable was cold and damp. The baby Jesus was wrapped in rags. The Bible says in Luke 2:7, *"She wrapped the baby with cloth and laid him in a feeding trough."* Also, perhaps the stable was smelly from the manure, moldy hay, and aroma of animals. Was this a sign of poverty, or was this due to the circumstances of the day? There just wasn't any room in the inn. The journey to Bethlehem was mandated by Emperor Caesar Augustus, the founder of the Roman Empire, when he sent out a decree for everyone to go back home to register for the census. Bethlehem was a small place and off the road from Jerusalem. The availability for a guest house or inn would have been limited.

> *…and she gave birth to her first child, a son. She wrapped him in cloth and laid him down in a feeding trough, because there was no space for them in the living-quarters.*
> *Luke 2:7 CJB (Complete Jewish Bible)*

According to Luke, the Greek word for living quarters in the above text is *kataluma*. This word is best described as a "guest room" in a private home versus a public place where travelers would use, such as an inn.[4] Joseph traveled to Bethlehem in Judea, his small ancestral hometown, where he had relatives. A good Jewish family would more than likely find a place for Mary, especially since she was pregnant, expecting her first-born son, had there been room. A typical Judean house would include a guest room in the back part of the house, or upstairs on a second floor, and lodging in the house for the household animals. When the time for Jesus' birth came, there were no rooms available because all the travelers had returned for the census (Luke 2:4-6). To keep warm and protect each other and their animals, Mary and Joseph slept downstairs in a common area near the door. This area had a manger for food and water for the animals brought in at night or during times when the weather was dreadful. Mary placed Jesus in a manger or feeding trough so that he might have a place to lie.

> *So, Joseph also went up from the town of Nazareth in Galilee to Judea, to Bethlehem the town of David, because he belonged to the house and line of David. He went*

---

[4] https://answersingenesis.org/holidays/christmas/christmas-no-room-for-an-inn/

> *there to register with Mary, who was pledged to be married to him and was expecting a child. <u>While they were there</u>, the time came for the baby to be born, and she gave birth to her firstborn, a son. She wrapped him in cloths and placed him in a manger, because there was no guest room available for them.*
> *Luke 2:4-6 NIV*

Another idea that has been mentioned was whether Jesus was born in a cave. Even though tradition has handed down the idea that Jesus' birthplace was in a stable, historical records have stated that Jesus could have been born in a cave. This is based on information found in records dating from the first century, where animals were also kept in caves. As stated above, the Bible does not give us any more information except that He was laid in a manger, and there was no guest room available for Him.

According to an article in Christianity.com, Bible scholars are less sure about the details involving the setting of Jesus' birth:

> The question of where Jesus was born is often answered with a city – Bethlehem. We know this from Biblical prophecies and narrative accounts like in Luke 2:4 and Matthew 2:1. But Bible scholars

are less sure about more specific details involving the setting. Again, we know from Luke's gospel where Jesus was *not* born – an inn because there wasn't room for his parents (see Luke 2:7, cited above). Was Jesus born in a cave? While this question is not much discussed in modern times, the tradition that connects a cave with Christ's birth is very ancient.[5]

> *So, Joseph also went up from the town of Nazareth in Galilee to Judea, to Bethlehem, the town of David, because he belonged to the house and line of David.*
> *Luke 2:4 NIV*
>
> *After Jesus was born in Bethlehem in Judea, during the time of King Herod, Magi from the east came to Jerusalem*
> *Matthew 2:1 NIV*
>
> *And she gave birth to her firstborn, a son. She wrapped him in cloths and placed him in a manger, because there was no guest room available for them.*
> *Luke 2:7 NIV*

---

[5] https://www.christianity.com/jesus/birth-of-jesus/bethlehem/was-jesus-born-in-a-cave.html

Magi – Wise Men

Magi, also known as wise men, from the east went to Jerusalem, traveling searching for the one born the king of the Jews (note the Bible does not say how many wise men visited nor reveal their names). While in Judea, the wise men inquired of King Herod as to the whereabouts of the child. Neither knew the exact location. However, according to the Scriptures, Micah 5:2 states that *"He would be born in Bethlehem Ephrathah."* As they left King Herod, the wise men saw the star they were following rise ahead of them. They journeyed until they saw the star rest, and there they found the Christ Child, Jesus. When they got to the house, they saw the child, bowed down and worshipped him, and they gave generous gifts of gold, frankincense, and myrrh in honor of Jesus (Matthew 2:11).

Meanwhile, King Herod, sometimes called "Herod the Great," king of Judea, became enraged because he was tricked by the magi. Previously, Herod had secretly called aside the wise men and instructed them to go and search diligently, and when they found Jesus, they were to report their findings back to him. Herod and all Jerusalem were troubled with the news of a new king, so they asked the magi to report the child's whereabouts, under the pretense that Herod wanted to go and worship Him also. When the wise men did not report back to him the exact location of the birth, Herod ordered the slaughtering of all the boys who were two years or younger born in and around Bethlehem. When word came that the governor of Judea was killing all the babies, Joseph was warned by an angel in a dream to take his family to Egypt. This was so that they could escape from the wrath of King Herod.

> *But thou, Bethlehem Ephrathah, which art little to be among the thousands of Judah, out of thee shall one come forth unto me that is to be ruler in Israel; whose goings forth are from of old, from everlasting.*
> *Micah 5:2 ASV*

> *On coming to the house, they saw the child with his mother Mary, and they bowed down and worshiped him. Then they opened their treasures and presented him with gifts of gold, frankincense and myrrh.*
> *Matthew 2:11 NIV*

Two thoughts regarding Jesus' birth:

1. We do not know when the Magi actually visited Jesus. We do know that it could not have been the night that Jesus was

> born. The Bible reveals that He was not a baby lying in a manger but a child, as stated in Matthew 2:11 (see above).
> 2. The time frame indicates that it could have been any time between 40 days and two years. The 40 days would mean that they arrived after the purification period for the mother. The two years would be referenced when King Herod ordered the killing of children two years or younger.

Wow, just think how you would have felt if you knew someone wanted to kill your son. I know you would do just about anything to keep your little one safe. Many times, God will use a dream to warn us of potential danger. Or perhaps, you may have thought, "Oh, I better go this way versus another," just to find out there was an accident on the road you did not take. When you have a strong feeling about something, God may be saying, "Follow my lead." Another saying I have heard is, "That was a close call." Yes, God was protecting you, and that's when we all should give thanks to God. Just as God protected Jesus from King Herod's hands, He will protect His children.

Homeless?

An article that appeared in the *Evangel Magazine* by Daniel Black entitled, 'Was Jesus Homeless and Poor?' indicates that Joseph and Mary were not homeless.

> *There is no evidence in the Gospels that Jesus was ever homeless. The issue here is not about whether or not Jesus owned a house. For 19 years, my family and I lived in church-furnished parsonages. We did not own a house, but we were not homeless.*[6]

When the governor of Judea died, Joseph and Mary returned with Jesus to their home in Nazareth. Throughout their journey, they observed the religious laws of the land. They did not become homeless, nor were they just wandering and begging. They were ordinary citizens in their community. Joseph was a skilled tradesman, a carpenter, and Mary a housewife looking after their home.

Whether you live in a house or an apartment, wherever you have made your home, remember, a home

---

[6] https://www.evangelmagazine.com/2017/03/was-jesus-homeless-and-poor/

is simply where you lay your head at night and rest. Just because you do not own a house does not mean you are poor. People have different priorities, and owning a house is not necessarily an important factor for happiness or determining wealth. Many view home ownership as a burden because of the upkeep of the entire property, internally and externally. Instead, remember to be content where God has you; your situation could likely worsen. Tomorrow is not promised, and if you die, you are not taking any of your possessions with you; you don't see a U-Haul at a funeral.

No Place to Lay

Matthew 8:19-20 and Luke 9:8 stated that *"Jesus did not have a place to lay His head."* This statement came when Jesus was speaking to a scribe that claimed he would follow Jesus wherever He went, as one of His disciples. Basically, Jesus was letting him know that there was a cost to living the lifestyle that Jesus chose. Jesus' lifestyle was more akin to homelessness. Unlike the scribes that were accustomed to a lifestyle of wealth and lavish homes, Jesus and his disciples would stay in the homes of those that provided a place for them. Jesus further compared His lifestyle to that of animals when He said, *"Foxes have dens and birds have nest, but the Son of Man has no place to lay his head* (Matthew 8:19-20)." Jesus emphasized the differences here so that the scribe could have a broader picture of what was expected when walking with Jesus. Also, Jesus wanted the scribe to know that there was no rest from responsibilities when following Him. During that time, people were anticipating an earthly leader, a king, to save them from the current political leadership, but Jesus' kingdom was not an earthly one but a heavenly kingdom. Today, Christians have many choices in serving God. Some become missionaries living in poor environments while others serve in other capacities in a wealthier environment. What is important is our willingness to give up everything for the kingdom of God. We are to put God first, above all else, with a sincere attitude. Before Jesus set out to minister, He lived with Joseph and Mary at the home they had in Nazareth. Once His public ministry began, Matthew 4:13 says, *"He lived in Capernaum."* Also, Jesus would stay with Martha, Mary, and Lazarus in Bethany, near Jerusalem. As stated earlier, many people offered Jesus a place to stay in their homes. Jesus may not have owned a house, but He was not homeless. When I think of a homeless person, I think of someone that does not have a home or job. Although some homeless people live in a shelter, the temporary nature of that situation prevents them from calling it home.

> *Then a teacher of the law came to him and said, "Teacher, I will follow you wherever you go." Jesus replied, "Foxes have dens and birds have nests, but the Son of Man has no place to lay his head."*
> *Matthew 8:19-20 NIV*

> *Jesus replied, "Foxes have dens and birds have nests, but the Son of Man has no place to lay his head."*
> *Luke 9:58 NIV*

Leaving Nazareth, he went and lived in Capernaum, which was by the lake in the area of Zebulun and Naphtali
 Matthew 4:13 NIV

Borrowed

When Jesus entered Jerusalem, He rode on a donkey that He borrowed. Jesus often borrowed things, boats, and even the tomb in which He was buried.

- Jesus Borrowed a Donkey, a Colt, the Foal of a Donkey

Jesus did not claim ownership for any earthly property, but He had access to whatever He needed. In fulfillment of the scripture found in Zechariah 9:9, when Jesus neared Jerusalem and came to Bethphage on the Mount of Olives, Jesus sent out two disciples. He told them to go into a nearby village and bring the colt tied at the village entrance and told them if they were asked why they were taking the colt, they were to say that the Lord needed it. When the disciples returned, they threw cloaks on the colt. Jesus sat on it and rode into Jerusalem. Many in the crowd, awaiting Jesus' arrival, threw their cloaks and spread leafy branches on the road before Him. They were cheering, *"Hosanna! Blessed is the One coming in the name of the Lord. Blessed is the coming kingdom of our father David. Hosanna in the highest [heavens]!"* (Mark 11:1-10).

You may ask, but why did Jesus ride a donkey? The significance is that a donkey is a humble, lowly animal that signifies peace, and riding it was a way to relate to the common people. Typically, in the Bible, to ride a prestigious horse was reserved for kings and in times of war. I have heard that perhaps riding on a colt was God's way of saying Jesus came as a king but to serve and save the oppressed, not conquer them. Jesus embraced the poor not only because He loved them but also because it was especially difficult for poor Jewish people to live under Roman rule.

> *Rejoice greatly, Daughter Zion! Shout, Daughter Jerusalem! See, your king comes to you, righteous and victorious, lowly and riding on a donkey, on a colt, the foal of a donkey.*
>
> *Zachariah 9:9 NIV*

> *As they approached Jerusalem and came to Bethphage and Bethany at the Mount of Olives, Jesus sent two of his disciples, saying to them, "Go to the village ahead of you, and just as you enter it, you will find a colt tied there, which no one has ever ridden. Untie it and bring it here. If anyone asks you, 'Why are you doing this?' say, 'The Lord needs it and will send it back here shortly.'"*

They went and found a colt outside in the street, tied at a doorway. As they untied it, some people standing there asked, "What are you doing, untying that colt?" They answered as Jesus had told them to, and the people let them go. When they brought the colt to Jesus and threw their cloaks over it, he sat on it. Many people spread their cloaks on the road, while others spread branches they had cut in the fields. Those who went ahead and those who followed shouted,

"Hosanna!"

"Blessed is he who comes in the name of the Lord!"

"Blessed is the coming kingdom of our father David!"

"Hosanna in the highest heaven!"
Mark 11:1-10 NIV

Life's Journey

- Jesus Borrows Boats

On a couple of occasions, while Jesus was preaching to large crowds of people, overcrowding forced Him to retreat to the edge of the lake to hear from God. As the people were waiting and yearning for the promised Messiah, He gained notoriety because of the many miracles He had performed. As a result, the crowds continued to grow. Jesus eventually had to move completely away from the multitude so as not to be overcome by the crowd. In the book of Luke, verses 5:1-3, we see Jesus on the shore by the Lake of Gennesaret. Jesus noticed two boats at the edge of the water left by fishermen as they were washing their fishing nets. Jesus stepped into one of the boats that belonged to Simon Peter and asked him to pull away from the shore. Jesus sat and taught the multitude of people from the boat.

> *One day as Jesus was standing by the Lake of Gennesaret, the people were crowding around him and listening to the word of God. He saw at the water's edge two boats, left there by the fishermen, who were washing their nets. He got into one of the boats, the one belonging to Simon, and asked him to put out a little from shore.*

> *Then he sat down and taught the people from the boat.*
> *Luke 5:1-3 NIV*

On another occasion, recorded in Mark 4:1, Jesus asked the disciples to get a boat ready near the shore of the Sea of Galilee in the event that the crowds became assertive and to keep the crowds from injuring Him. In Mark 3:7, we see that the crowds expanded across Israel, including Judea, Jerusalem, Idumea, the Jordan region, and around Tyre and Sidon. The increase resulted from people hearing of Jesus' healing power and all that He was doing. They too wanted to experience Jesus, just as we want.

> *Again, Jesus began to teach by the lake. The crowd that gathered around him was so large that he got into a boat and sat in it out on the lake, while all the people were along the shore at the water's edge.*
> *Mark 4:1 NIV*

> *Jesus withdrew with his disciples to the lake, and a large crowd from Galilee followed. When they heard about all he was doing, many people came to him from Judea, Jerusalem, Idumea, and*

> *the regions across the Jordan and around Tyre and Sidon. Because of the crowd he told his disciples to have a small boat ready for him, to keep the people from crowding him.*
>
> *Mark 3:7 NIV*

Even though we do not see Jesus physically, He is attentively waiting for us to call on Him. Just like the multitude that wanted to hear what Jesus had to say, we too should do the same. The difference is that we have the Word of God, the Bible, in which Jesus speaks to us today. What He said to the people then is still relevant today and is spoken through His Word. Wouldn't it be wonderful if multitudes of people eagerly rushed to the church to hear the Word of God? This reminds me of when I first became a Christian, I would say, "All week, God, you came to my house, and now I want to go to your house on Sunday." Going to church to celebrate our Lord God Almighty is what pleases Him. Let's spread the word. Jesus is the same yesterday, today, and forever.

- Jesus Buried in a Borrowed Tomb

The tomb in which Jesus was buried was borrowed from a rich member of the Jewish council, an influential man, and a supporter of Jesus. His name was

Joseph, and he was a man from the Judean town of Arimathea. Joseph and Nicodemus, both members of the Jewish council, took Jesus' body down from the cross and carried Him to a new tomb where His body was wrapped in long strips of cloth. Nicodemus took a mixture of spices, myrrh, and aloes, enough fit for a king, and poured it on Jesus' body (Luke 23:50-56 & John 19:37). Jesus' body was buried according to the Jewish burial customs in which dead bodies could not be left exposed overnight. You may ask the question, why was Jesus buried in a borrowed tomb? Well, Jesus knew what was coming up next. He knew that this was not His permeant home and that He would be resurrected and alive forevermore. There was no need to buy a tomb that would be used for such a short time.

> *Now there was a man named Joseph, a member of the Council, a good and upright man, who had not consented to their decision and action. He came from the Judean town of Arimathea, and he himself was waiting for the kingdom of God. Going to Pilate, he asked for Jesus' body. Then he took it down, wrapped it in linen cloth and placed it in a tomb cut in the rock, one in*

*which no one had yet been laid.
It was Preparation Day, and the
Sabbath was about to begin.*

*The women who had come with
Jesus from Galilee followed Joseph
and saw the tomb and how his
body was laid in it.*

Luke 23:50-56 NIV

*He was accompanied by Nicodemus,
the man who earlier had visited
Jesus at night. Nicodemus brought a
mixture of myrrh and aloes, about
seventy-five pounds. Taking Jesus'
body, the two of them wrapped it,
with the spices, in strips of linen.
This was in accordance with Jewish
burial customs.*

John 19:39 NIV

Taxes

A saying that we have all heard for many years is, "In life's journey, there are two things we can count on, paying taxes and dying." In Romans 13:1, Jesus taught that we must be subject to the governing authorities, noting that God has established these authorities. According to Titus 3:1, the Bible instructs us to be obedient to the governing authorities and be ready for every good work. We may not always agree with the laws passed by mere mortals, especially when we have moral objections (one example is the legalization of abortion). We are to personally refrain from such laws when they do not align with the word of God. The scriptures tell us that the sanctity of human life should be preserved. Every life is precious in the eyes of God, and every person is valuable and uniquely created by Him (Acts 17:24-25).

> *Let everyone be subject to the governing authorities, for there is no authority except that which God has established. The authorities that exist have been established by God.*
>
> *Romans 13:1 NIV*

> *Remind them to be submissive to rulers and authorities, to be obedient, to be ready for every good work.*
> *Titus 3:1 ESV*

> *The God who made the world and everything in it, being Lord of heaven and earth, does not live-in temples made by man, nor is he served by human hands, as though he needed anything, since he himself gives to all mankind life and breath and everything.*
> *Acts 17:24-25 ASV*

In the interest of keeping the peace and honoring the authorities in place, Jesus encouraged his followers to pay the taxes due to Rome. Jesus knew the Pharisees were trying to trap Him, and He did not want to give them any ammunition to use against Him. When it was time to pay the temple taxes, Jesus told Simon to cast a line into the lake to get the money needed to pay their taxes. Simon was to take the first fish that he caught, for in the fishes' mouth, he would find a four-drachma coin (each person was to pay two-drachma) to pay the taxes due for Jesus and himself.

> *"But so that we may not cause offense, go to the lake and throw out your line. Take the first fish you catch; open its mouth and you will find a four-drachma coin. Take it and give it to them for my tax and yours."*
>
> *Matthew 17:27 NIV*

When governing authorities impose higher taxes, it is unfortunate that everyone is subject to the said rate. We may not want to pay them or believe it is fair, but we are responsible for paying them no matter what. One thing we can count on, if we do not pay our taxes now, the penalties will add up really fast, and we will end up paying even more, sooner or later.

Crucified but not Dead

When Jesus' earthly ministry came to an end, the religious leaders were jealous and hated Jesus. They were jealous because they felt He was a threat to their way of life, as Jesus attracted larger crowds that wanted to hear more about God and His teachings. Jesus taught the multitudes to love God and to love one another. The established religious leaders taught 'about' God, but not how to love God. The chief priest and the Pharisees were afraid that Jesus' teachings were a threat to their power, and the more people believed in Jesus, meant fewer followers for them. The Pharisees became fearful that the Romans would take away their temple and nation if their roles were diminished (John 11:47-48). They also hated Jesus because of His unwillingness to follow their religious traditions. Jesus exposed them as hypocrites, caring more for their traditions and laws than Biblical values such as justice, mercy, and faithfulness (Matthew 23:23). Jesus' ministry was primarily targeted at the poor, as He had compassion for them. This was evident when He healed the sick, gave sight to the blind, and cared for the oppressed.

> *Then the chief priests and the Pharisees called a meeting of the Sanhedrin. If we let him go on like this, everyone will believe in*

> *him, and then the Romans will come and take away both our temple and our nation."*
>
> *John 11:47-48 NIV*

> *"Woe to you, teachers of the law and Pharisees, you hypocrites! You give a tenth of your spices-- mint, dill and cumin. But you have neglected the more important matters of the law--justice, mercy and faithfulness. You should have practiced the latter, without neglecting the former.*
>
> *Matthew 23:23 NIV*

Basically, Jesus went from a position of Sovereignty to servanthood. I believe that God wants us to have an abundant life filled with His peace, love, and the provisions for all our needs. Our focus should not be on what we have but on the will of God, which is servanthood and preaching the Gospel. Jesus may have lived like a poor person, but in reality, He had everything He needed.

His teaching was met with ridicule and insults, and the governing leaders, the Sanhedrin, Pontius Pilate, and the Romans, were instrumental in His crucifixion.

Life's Journey

After Jesus was crucified, He was buried, but death could not keep Him in the grave. He arose from the grave to return to His heavenly home. Before His return, he appeared to many of his followers. In John 16:28, Jesus encouraged the disciples to continue His mission when He revealed to them that He was going back to the Father in heaven. In Matthew 28:16-17, the disciples saw Jesus when they went to Galilee (as Jesus had instructed them to do). In Acts 1:2-3, Luke's address to Theophilus recounts Jesus' numerous appearances to his disciples, giving them many convincing proofs that He was alive. He appeared to them for forty days. In Acts 1:6-11, Jesus informed the disciples that they would receive power when the Holy Spirit came upon them and that they would be Jesus' witness to the ends of the world. After all this, Jesus was taken up to heaven as witnessed by the disciples. He ascended to be with the Father in all His glory. Jesus now sits at the right hand of the Father (Mark 16:19).

> *I came from the Father and entered the world; now I am leaving the world and going back to the Father."*
>
> *John 16;28 NIV*
>
> *Then the eleven disciples went to Galilee, to the mountain where Jesus had told them to go. When*

they saw him, they worshiped him; but some doubted.
Matthew 28:16-17 NIV

Until the day he was taken up to heaven, after giving instructions through the Holy Spirit to the apostles he had chosen. After his suffering, he presented himself to them and gave many convincing proofs that he was alive. He appeared to them over a period of forty days and spoke about the kingdom of God.
Acts 1:2-3 NIV

Then they gathered around him and asked him, "Lord, are you at this time going to restore the kingdom to Israel?" He said to them: "It is not for you to know the times or dates the Father has set by his own authority. But you will receive power when the Holy Spirit comes on you; and you will be my witnesses in Jerusalem, and in all Judea and Samaria, and to the ends of the earth." After he said this, he was taken up before their very eyes, and a cloud hid him from their sight. They were looking intently up into the sky as he was going, when suddenly two men dressed in white stood beside them. "Men of Galilee," they said, "why do you stand here looking into the sky? This same Jesus, who has been taken from you into heaven, will come back in the same way you have seen him go into heaven."

Acts 1:6-11 NIV

After the Lord Jesus had spoken to them, he was taken up into heaven and he sat at the right hand of God.

Mark 16-19 NIV

Philippians 2:6-11 summarizes Jesus' life on earth as preaching the good news (the Gospel message). My favorite part is, "Who (Jesus), being the very nature God, did not consider equality with God to be used to His own advantage; rather, he made himself nothing by taking the very nature of a servant, being made in human likeness." This shows how much God loves us. He sent His only Son to an unmerited people to save them from eternal destruction. He offers us this free gift of eternal life in Christ Jesus, an eternal life filled with God's grace, mercy, favor, and a personal relationship with him now and forever.

> *Who, being in very nature God, did not consider equality with God something to be used to his own advantage; rather, he made himself nothing by taking the very nature of a servant, being made in human likeness. And being found in appearance as a man, he humbled himself by becoming obedient to death — even death on a cross! Therefore, God exalted him to the highest place and gave him the name that is above every name, that at the name of Jesus every knee should bow, in heaven and on earth and under the earth, and every tongue acknowledge that Jesus Christ is Lord, to the glory of God the Father.*
> *Philippians 2:6-11 NIV*

This can be a hard concept to comprehend. Just think of how you would feel if your friend, who loves you unconditionally, is put to death because of people that hate Him and are jealous of His popularity. Your friend's life mission was to offer everyone a life filled with God's peace, not just for now but through eternity. Unfortunately, people only want power and to control others. They want everyone to live according to their own agenda. When people refuse to let the power-hungry control them, they are met with bullying and deceit. Lies are spread to try to discredit them, and they may even be put to death. This is exactly what happened to Jesus. Fortunately, this isn't the end of the story. Jesus' death, resurrection, and how He returned to meet with the Disciples proves that not only is He still alive, but it assures us that one day He is coming back for us, His children.

Chapter 4

God Uses the Weak

As we see throughout the Bible, God uses weak people to lead others to Himself and demonstrate His glory. He uses ordinary people to accomplish extraordinary tasks. We might say, "I don't have anything special that God would even consider using me." Don't kid yourself. God can use all of us, especially those with a willing heart. God uses the weak to show His power and so that He alone gets the glory (2 Corinthians 4:7). When we humble ourselves, acknowledging our weaknesses, God can then use our weaknesses to strengthen us as we depend upon Him. We recognize a need for a savior when there is no other way to turn. The Bible is filled with examples, showing us that God can equip any of us to do His work in building His kingdom. He uses the weak because we are humbled in our weakness, knowing that God used us and thus blessed us. When others are blessed, this gives us hope knowing we too can trust God.

*All surpassing power is from God
and not from us.*
2 Corinthians 4:7 NIV

There are many examples of ordinary people in the Bible that God used. They are people just like you and me, who felt that they had nothing to offer. Now, let's take a look at some of these individuals.

- Let's start with Adam and Eve in the book of Genesis. God blessed them and gave them everything they would need. He gave them dominion over all living things. But they conceded to the serpent's temptation when they ate from the forbidden tree, the tree of good and evil, and thus caused the fall of man. Even though they were weak and failed, God still used them for his eternal purposes. To clothe Adam and Eve, the first animal was killed. This initial sacrifice showed them that to save the world; a perfect sacrifice would be needed. The only one qualified to make this sacrifice is Jesus Christ.

You have probably heard the saying, "You don't know what you have until you lose it." This is the biggest example I can think of where a couple had everything handed to them and then lost it. I would be kicking myself to think I was so foolish to have lost everything. Because of their disobedience, the hardship that followed continues today with weeds, thorns, and painful child birthing. Living in the desert, even when it does not rain, the weeds grow with a vengeance while other plants struggle to say alive. Yes, Adam and Eve, we will always remember you.

- Abraham was very old, but his faith did not waiver. He trusted God's Word when God promised him that he would make him into a great nation. Elderly, he and his wife Sarah were well beyond childbearing age, not to mention that Sarah was barren, yet their son Isaac was born when he was 100 years of age. Through his lineage, the greatest offspring that came about was that of Jesus Christ. Sometimes, God's timing is not what we hope for, but God uses even the elderly to accomplish His eternal plan. Because of Sarah's age, this could have only happened by a miracle of God. To God be the glory!

At 71, I cannot imagine starting over with a newborn. Just thinking about the feedings, diapers, and perhaps sleepless nights makes me realize just how much Sarah had to face at her age. I am sure that since this was her first son, these tiresome duties were replaced with the abundance of joy she had over finally holding a child of her own. Funny how this works; while going through the feedings and changing diapers, I did not mind it at all, but when I no longer had to prepare bottles of formula or change diapers, I was delighted.

- Jacob was a liar. He was a shifty, untrustworthy cheater, and his character was associated with trickery and deception. He stole the birthright from his older twin brother Esau using these methods. He even showed favoritism among his sons. Joseph was his favorite, causing hatred amongst his other sons, and it resulted in the continuation of deceit behavior when the brothers sold Joseph into slavery. Before they returned home, they wanted to make it appear that Joseph had been killed, so they planned to deceive their father. Genesis 36:31-33 records these events, *"Then they got Joseph's beautiful robe. They killed a goat and dipped the robe in the blood. They took it back to their father. They said, "We found this. Take a look at it. See if it's your son's robe." Jacob recognized it. He said, "It's my son's robe! A wild animal has eaten him up. Joseph must have been torn to pieces."* Though Jacob was a trickster, once he acknowledged his need for God, God blessed his life. God blessed him with many children and made him the father of the twelve tribes of Israel through his sons: Ruben, Simeon, Levi, Judah, Zebulun, Issachar, Dan, Gad, Asher, Naphtali, Joseph, and Benjamin. In the book of Numbers, the list of the tribes does not name Levi (the Levites) because they were responsible for the priestly duties. You will notice, too, that the tribe of Joseph in Numbers is also missing because Ephraim and Manasseh represent it. See Numbers 1:4-15.

One man from each tribe, each of them the head of his family, is to help you. These are the names of the men who are to assist you:
from Reuben, Elizur son of Shedeur;
from Simeon, Shelumiel son of Zurishaddai;
from Judah, Nahshon son of Amminadab;
from Issachar, Nethanel son of Zuar;
from Zebulun, Eliab son of Helon;
from the sons of Joseph:
from Ephraim, Elishama son of Ammihud;
from Manasseh, Gamaliel son of Pedahzur;

from Benjamin, Abidan son of Gideoni;
from Dan, Ahiezer son of Ammishaddai;
from Asher, Pagiel son of Okran;
from Gad, Eliasaph son of Deuel;
from Naphtali, Ahira son of Enan."
Numbers 1:4-15 NIV

Even the most unlikely of people who outwardly spoke against God have made a 180° turn and have become the greatest promoters of the Gospel of Jesus. Jacob may have started out deceiving others, but God used him anyway. God blessed him with many children and made him the father of many tribes through his sons. We may feel like a lost cause and ruled by our sinful nature, but when we turn to God, asking for forgiveness and repent, God blesses us and lifts us out of the mire.

- When God commissioned Moses to lead His people, the Israelites, to the promised land, Moses pleaded with God to find someone else. He said that he did not have eloquent speaking abilities, that he was slow in speech and slow in tongue. God had compassion on His people because of the oppression they endured under Pharaoh in Egypt. Thus, He sent Moses to lead them out of slavery. However, because of Moses' hesitation, God sent Aaron, his brother, along with him to speak for Moses. The Israelites challenged them with their disbelief and constant complaining, even though God had provided everything they needed. Despite these difficulties, Moses was not deterred from leading the Israelites to the promised land.

The feeling of inadequacy or unworthiness can cause one to hesitate, and at times lose out on the blessings of God. When God calls us to perform a job, He equips us to accomplish the given task. We only need to put our trust in Him, knowing that when He calls us to do a job, He will always be there to give us a hand. This is especially true when we feel we are stuck. An encouraging word and reminder of this truth is found in Philippians 1:6 when God says, *"He who begins a good work in us will carry us to completion."*

> *being confident of this, that he who began a good work in you will carry it on to completion until the day of Christ Jesus.*
> *Philippians 1:6 NIV*

There have been times in my life when I have witnessed other people stepping in to assist with the needs of others, and I always said, "I wish I had thought to do that." Other times, I have thought about doing something, but hesitated and then it was too late to follow through. I regret that I was too slow. I believe that God may put opportunities in our minds to do something, but we may fail to follow through and lose out on blessings. The closer we walk with God, the more we hear God's voice. Sometimes, when we think of a way to bless others or when others may tell us about a need, like Moses, our reluctance to respond rapidly may result from a lack of confidence in ourselves. When we serve others in need, whether financially, giving our time, or physically helping them, Jesus promises to reward us. As stated in Luke 6:38, *"He will give a good measure and running over."* I have heard several people say, and I believe this, that we cannot out-give God.

> *Give, and it will be given to you. A good measure, pressed down, shaken together and running over, will be poured into your lap. For with the measure you use, it will be measured to you."*
> *Luke 6:38 NIV*

- Noah walked in obedience with God and built the Ark, according to the specification God commanded, resulting in the salvation of his family, mankind, and animals. The mission was met with ridicule as everyone around him thought he was crazy and did not listen to him. When the rain poured, the people wanted to go into the Ark, but it was too late, as God had already shut the door. It rained for 40 days and 40 nights, but they were in the Ark for just a little over a year. After the flood, Noah became a farmer and planted a vineyard, which produced wine. Unfortunately, he became drunk one night and fell asleep naked inside his tent. His son Ham found him, and his brother walked backward in order not to see his nakedness, covering him on the way out.

Noah's trust in God was unwavering. He demonstrated this when he was obedient to build the Ark. Noah had never seen rain, so why would he build an Ark? The unknown did not deter him from following the command and will of God. He proceeded with the job at hand until it was completed; now that is faith. Unfortunately, him getting drunk and being found naked by his son Ham brought shame to his family, as Ham gossiped about his father.

When a brother falls, we should remember that just like Noah, we all have a weak side, including you and me. The decisions we make carry consequences, sometimes good, sometimes bad. This is why it is important to choose wisely. One bad choice can destroy the reputation of any of us. Instead of ridiculing people, we should have compassion because even the most godly man or woman can stumble.

- Jonah ran from God when commissioned to preach repentance to Nineveh. The Ninevites were wicked, idolatrous, and rebellious people, and Jonah was sent to warn them of their impending doom (judgment). Instead, Jonah, who was a prophet and servant of God, fled in the opposite direction in disobedience to God until he met with a great fish. After being swallowed by a fish, Jonah cried out to God for mercy. After Jonah repents, God extends his mercy and love by causing the fish to throw Jonah up on the shore. God, the God of second chances, and sometimes many more, gives Jonah another chance. Jonah went to Nineveh to preach the word, as God had directed him. This generation of Ninevites repented and were saved from their wicked ways.

When I read this story, one thought that comes to mind is how merciful God is to his children. Jonah was a prophet of God, and we can say he should have known better than to run from God. Yet, God, in His mercy and love, gives Jonah a second chance. The second chance was not just meant for Jonah, but God's will was to save the people in Nineveh from their wicked ways. You see, God will give us, as He did with Nineveh, second chances because of His love for us. He does not want anyone to perish.

- Rahab was a prostitute, Canaanite, and a liar, and yet, she is considered a biblical heroine. Although she is often called "Rahab the harlot," she is an ancestor of Jesus! In the lineage of Jesus, found in Matthew 1:5, her name is among those listed. As a Canaanite, she was an enemy of God's people, hated by Israel. She lived in Jericho, the promised land, and assisted the Israelites in taking over the city. She hid two Hebrew spies on her roof under some stalks of flax to protect them from being captured.

Furthermore, she lied about their whereabouts when questioned by the Canaanites. Thus, God extended favor to her, and she survived the conquering of Jericho. She and her family were saved because of what she did.

The Genealogy of Jesus the Messiah
⁵Salmon the father of Boaz, whose mother was Rahab, Boaz the

*father of Obed, whose mother was
Ruth, Obed the father of Jesse,*
Matthew 1:5 NIV

Rahab may have been a harlot, but she was shrewd and showed bravery when she hid the two spies and lied about their whereabouts. They were the enemy and hated by the Canaanites, so you may ask why would she even consider helping them? Rahab had heard about what God was doing for His people, the many miracles He had performed (e.g., when God dried up the water of the Red Sea), and how God had promised the land to them. So, she hid the two spies, but only after first agreeing with them. She made them swear to her with a promise from the Lord to return the favor. The spies promised to remember her and her entire family by sparing their lives when Jericho was conquered (Joshua 2:9-13).

> *Before the spies lay down for the night, she went up on the roof and said to them, "I know that the LORD has given you this land and that a great fear of you has fallen on us, so that all who live in this country are melting in fear because of you. We have heard how the LORD dried up the water of the Red Sea for you when you came*

out of Egypt, and what you did to Sihon and Og, the two kings of the Amorites east of the Jordan, whom you completely destroyed. When we heard of it, our hearts melted in fear and everyone's courage failed because of you, for the LORD your God is God in heaven above and on the earth below. "Now then, please swear to me by the LORD that you will show kindness to my family, because I have shown kindness to you. Give me a sure sign that you will spare the lives of my father and mother, my brothers and sisters, and all who belong to them —and that you will save us from death."
Joshua 2:9-13 NIV

- Just an ordinary boy's lunch of two small fish and five small barley loaves of bread was used to feed the multitude of 5,000 men, plus women and children. Everyone ate plenty, with food leftover, enough to fill 12 baskets.

A simple story, but just think about when you have made your lunch for school or work. You only made enough for one, right? So, I am sure that these children took what they thought would be enough food for perhaps one day. Yet, miraculously, Jesus fed thousands of men plus the women and children. God often does the extraordinary so that there is no doubt that it had to be a miracle only He could perform. When God extends the same favor to us, often, people do not acknowledge God nor give Him thanks because pride gets in the way. God uses ordinary people to accomplish His goals. God often uses people to perform healings, but the real healer is God. We know that we alone cannot perform unforeseen miracles, and we should remember that the glory goes to God and God alone.

- Martha was a worrier. She snapped at Jesus when her sister Mary was not helping her with the preparations she was making for their guests. They had opened their home to Jesus, travelers, and his disciples. As Martha hurriedly made the preparations for the guests, Mary sat at Jesus's feet and listened as He taught.

When we invite a crowd over, for instance, when preparing for a wedding in which many jobs need to be done before the guests arrive, we enlist the help of others, and rightfully so. In the story of Mary and Martha, Jesus is not saying that if we make a promise to help, it is okay to break our promise. What He is saying is that, in this case,

Mary had chosen the right thing to do, and that was to listen and absorb every word that Jesus spoke while He was still here on earth. Jesus knew that Martha and Mary loved Him, but that was not the problem here. Humanly, Mary was a worrier, attending over the business of making sure the preparations for the gathering were done on time. Knowing that Martha was a worrier, Jesus was saying that we need to align our priorities by putting God, Jesus, first in our lives. Trade worry and anxiety with faith and peace by spending time in the presence of God. When we spend time with Jesus, we receive peace as we put our trust in Him. This story is found in Luke 10:38-42.

> *As Jesus and his disciples were on their way, he came to a village where a woman named Martha opened her home to him. She had a sister called Mary, who sat at the Lord's feet listening to what he said. But Martha was distracted by all the preparations that had to be made. She came to him and asked, "Lord, don't you care that my sister has left me to do the work by myself? Tell her to help me!"*

"Martha, Martha," the Lord answered, "you are worried and upset about many things, but few things are needed—or indeed only one. Mary has chosen what is better, and it will not be taken away from her."
Luke 10:38-42 NIV

- The Samaritan woman had a reputation as a sexually immoral sinner. She was the woman that Jesus ministered to while at Jacob's well. God used her as a witness to others, drawing people to Himself.

On the journey to Galilee, Jesus had to go through Sychar, Samaria, where Jacob's well was located. Tired from walking a long journey, Jesus sat on the curb of the well. The Samaritan woman approached, and Jesus asked her for a drink of water. Since Jesus was a Jew and she was a Samaritan, she questioned Him because Jews did not associate with Samaritans. She came to believe that Jesus was a prophet when He exposed her lifestyle, recounting that she had been married five times and was currently living with someone who was not her husband. Jesus continued to teach her about God the Father when He responded to her question regarding where the appropriate place to worship God was. He answered, *"Woman, believe me, a time is coming when you will worship the Father neither on this mountain nor in Jerusalem. You Samaritans worship what you do not know; we worship what we do know, for salvation is from the Jews. Yet a time is coming and has now come when the true worshipers will worship the Father in the Spirit and in truth, for they are the kind of worshipers the Father seeks. God is spirit, and his worshipers must worship in the Spirit and in truth"* (John 4:21-24 NIV). Realizing that Jesus could be the Messiah, she returned to her town and told the people what happened. She explained that Jesus knew all about her lifestyle before she had spoken a word to Him. The people went to see for themselves, and many Samaritans believed because of the woman's testimony.

This story tells me that if God can use a sexually immoral woman to lead others to the truths found in the Bible, then God can use any of us. Our past may be filled with stories we do not want others to know about or, worse, repeated, yet, God can use any circumstance to accomplish His goal to draw people to Himself, have fellowship with us, and save us from eternal damnation. If you are still alive, God can use you.

- Zacchaeus was a sinful man. Despite being a leading tax collector in the city, He was corrupt, collecting more taxes than he should have. When he heard that

Jesus, who he thought was a prophet, was passing through the city, he ran ahead of the people to get a better view. Because of his short stature, he climbed a sycamore tree allowing him to see Jesus. Jesus called him out, and he immediately came down. Jesus told Zacchaeus that He needed to stay with him. The most important part of this story is that Zacchaeus had a life-changing encounter with Jesus because of Jesus' compassion for sinners.

> *"Zacchaeus, come down immediately. I must stay at your house today."* [6] *So he came down at once and welcomed him gladly.*
> *Luke 19:5 NIV*

Now imagine a rich, corrupt tax collector who the people despised because of his excessive demands, hovering over them as they were already stretched financially. Jesus asked Zacchaeus to come down, and He said He would stay with Zacchaeus. The people grumbled and could not understand why Jesus would associate with him, a devious man. But Zacchaeus, on the other hand, was touched, and when he stood up, he declared:

> *"Look, Lord! Here and now, I give half of my possessions to the poor,*

> *and if I have cheated anybody out of anything, I will pay back four times the amount." Luke 19:8 NIV.*

Zacchaeus' repentant spirit was evident in his willingness to give half of his possessions to the poor and return all the money he had stolen with interest. This made Jesus happy. Jesus explained to the people that Zacchaeus and his household had come to salvation because of his faith. Jesus further responded to the grumblers that the very reason He had come to earth was to seek and save the lost (Luke 19:10 & Luke 5:31). Jesus said, *"I have not come to call the righteous, but sinners to repentance."*

> *"For the Son of Man came to seek and to save the lost."*
> Luke 19:10 NIV)

> *Jesus answered them, "It is not the healthy who need a doctor, but the sick. I have not come to call the righteous, but sinners to repentance."*
> *Luke 5:31 NIV*

- Simon (Peter) - The disciples also displayed times of weakness. Simon (Peter), one of the twelve disciples of Jesus, was a particularly close companion to Jesus, along with James and John. Despite their close relationship, he denied knowing Jesus 3 times. After the soldiers and religious leaders arrested Jesus, Peter was asked by a servant girl if he was with Jesus. Peter denied that he was one of Jesus' disciples. When asked again, he denied Jesus two more times. Just as Jesus foretold, the rooster crowed after Peter denied Him. When Jesus returned after the resurrection, Jesus not only affirmed his love for Simon Peter but appointed him chief apostle and leader of the first New Testament church. Peter was one of the most influential Christian leaders in the First Century.

Simon had betrayed his best friend, his Messiah. Can you imagine how he must have felt? Some of you have grown up with a childhood friend, and you think highly of them. One day, you do the unimaginable, which puts a big strain on your relationship; you think you blew it. But instead, your friend comes back and tells you that they understand and forgive you. You realize that your friend has given you a second chance, and you are thankful. That's exactly how Simon Peter felt when Jesus reaffirmed their relationship, and he was given a second chance to spread the good news of Jesus

Christ. He ended up becoming one of the most influential leaders in history. Yes, Jesus still gives second chances (and more) when we repent and ask for forgiveness.

- Thomas (Doubting Thomas) - When Jesus returned after the resurrection, Thomas, one of the twelve disciples, was not present with the others when Jesus appeared to them. When the disciples told Thomas that they had seen the Lord, he did not believe them. Instead, he stated, "Unless I see in his hands the mark of the nails, and place my finger on the mark of the nails, and place my hand on his side, I will never believe" (John 20:24-29).

Now Thomas (also known as Didymus), one of the Twelve, was not with the disciples when Jesus came. So the other disciples told him, "We have seen the Lord!"

But he said to them, "Unless I see the nail marks in his hands and put my finger where the nails were, and put my hand into his side, I will not believe."

> *A week later his disciples were in the house again, and Thomas was with them. Though the doors were locked, Jesus came and stood among them and said, "Peace be with you!" Then he said to Thomas, "Put your finger here; see my hands. Reach out your hand and put it into my side. Stop doubting and believe."*
>
> *Thomas said to him, "My Lord and my God!"*
>
> *Then Jesus told him, "Because you have seen me, you have believed; blessed are those who have not seen and yet have believed."*
> *John 20:24-29 NIV*

With our words, we can make statements that are taken out of context and or accidentally mislead. Of the twelve original Apostles of Jesus Christ, the one that was the most steadfast, loyal, mature, faith-filled, and courageous with vision was Thomas. Yet, he was unjustly judged over one statement that he made. He was known for checking the facts before he would believe. He was not with the other disciples when Jesus visited them; therefore, he needed to verify that Jesus had indeed really come back. When people hear rumors, the facts may not be accurate, so we need to diligently investigate before we repeat what we hear. In the same way, Thomas investigated the facts about Jesus' resurrection because he knew that Jesus had promised to return. So, a man of strong faith and belief in Jesus was wrongfully judged and did not deserve the title of Doubting Thomas.

- One of the original 12 disciples, Judas Iscariot, betrayed Jesus, his Master, by turning Him over to the authorities for 30 pieces of silver. Judas led the temple guard to Gethsemane and then identified Jesus by kissing him.

His actions ultimately led to the arrest of Jesus for heresy and His crucifixion.

Judas, one of the disciples, lived with and followed Jesus for three years. He was the appointed treasurer and a thief. He would help himself to what was put into the money bag. Judas walked and studied under the leadership of Jesus and became a close friend. His spiritual gifts included: healing, preaching, and exorcising demons. When the time came for the betrayal, he was bribed with a mere 30 pieces of silver. The Jewish soldiers had a pre-arranged agreement for Judas to kiss the one they were looking for. Jesus was inevitably condemned.

Judas, realizing what he had done, showed remorse and tried to return the 30 pieces of silver. The Jewish priests, however, refused to accept the money because it was considered blood money. What we do know is that Judas died shortly after that. There are two ideas as to how he met his death. Perhaps memories were confused or similar to when two people see an accident; their stories often contradict each other. After Judas threw the money back into the temple, he left. The first theory as to what happened after that stems from Matthew 27:5. We are told that Judas hanged himself. The second theory stems from Acts 1:18, where we are told that Judas took the money, bought a field, and fell on his head before he died.

> *So, Judas threw the money into the temple and left. Then he went away and hanged himself.*
> *Matthew 27:5 NIV*

> *(With the payment he received for his wickedness, Judas bought a field; there he fell headlong, his body burst open and all his intestines spilled out.*
> *Acts 1:18 NIV*

Unfortunately, the scriptures tell us that he had shown remorse, emotional remorse, filled with guilt and despair and not repentance from his sin. We know that God had a plan to allow His only Son to be sacrificed so that we can have the assurance of salvation. This is a free gift that all of us, individually, must verbally accept. The people that God uses are not always honest, God-fearing people; in fact, he uses the severest conditions to accomplish His sovereign will.

- Peter, James, and John – These three disciples could not stay awake for even one hour. In Matthew 26:40, when Jesus and His disciples went to the Garden of Gethsemane, Jesus went away from them to pray privately to His Father, asking the disciples to keep watch while He was gone, He prayed, *"My Father if it is possible, may this cup be taken from Me. Yet not as I will, but as You will"* (Matthew 26:39). When Jesus returned to the disciples, Peter, James, and John were asleep. He said to them, "Were you not able to keep watch with Me for one hour" (Matthew 26:40)?

Then he returned to his disciples and found them sleeping. "Couldn't you men keep watch with me for one hour?" he asked Peter.
Matthew 26:40 NIV

There is a saying I have heard many times; when a pastor is asked how many people the sanctuary holds, he responds with, "It sleeps…." To me, this is interesting to think how some people can go to church, and as soon as the preacher begins, they fall asleep. You may ask, "Why?" I believe there are many reasons. Some people go to church out of obligation, saying, "We go because we are supposed to go." But that's not the purpose of going to church. It should be a time where you look forward to being in the house of the Lord. Just like when you are at a friend's house, talking, laughing, or having a meal when you go to church, God wants us awake and vigilant and to be ready to talk to Him, praise and worship Him. We should be eager to learn as the pastor gives his sermon and uplift each other as we follow His leading. When we engage at church, He will equip us to serve Him and others throughout the week.

God continues to use people today to accomplish His plan to draw us to Himself.

Often, when we perceive that someone would be the most unlikely person, God sees a servant's heart that He can trust. Just like the front of a beautiful tapestry, God sees the finished product. We may only see the back of the tapestry, which looks messy—lacking precision because it is filled with knots and loose threads. Once it is weaved together, however, the colorful threads and textures come alive, displaying the glory of the Master's handiwork. Some people may be weak or perhaps have been through a challenging time in which someone else would have given up the hope of accomplishing their dreams, yet, they continue forward.

There are many others stories in the Bible, and throughout history; people displayed weakness, yet God used them for his kingdom. This should encourage us and give us confidence, knowing that God does not use perfect, strong, and better-qualified people, but rather, people who are willing to accept the task God offers. We can also find comfort in knowing that what God started He will carry to completion (Philippians 1:6). God doesn't have favorites; what He has done for others, He can do for us.

> *Being confident of this, that he who began a good work in you will carry it on to completion until the day of Christ Jesus.*
> *Philippians 1:6 NIV*

Chapter 5

Redemption

- Mephibosheth

The story of Mephibosheth is an example of redemption found in the Old Testament of the Bible. Let's begin this story with Israel's first king. King Saul had four sons with his wife Ahinoam: Jonathan was the oldest son, shvi (Abinadab), Malchi-shua, and Ish-bosheth (Esbaal), as well as two daughters, Merab and Michal (plus another child from his Concubine). His son Jonathan had a son by the name of Mephibosheth, Saul's grandson. Mephibosheth had a son by the name of Micha or Mica. Jonathan's best friend, who is like a brother, in fact, was Israel's 2nd King, David. These stories are found in the Old Testament in I and II Samuel.

When the Philistine army assembled for battle at the Israelites camp by Mount Gilboa in the Jezreel Valley, Saul became afraid, and terror filled his heart.

The fighting became intense as the Philistines were in direct pursuit of Saul, his sons, and the Israelite army. Three of Saul's sons, Jonathan, Abinadab, and Malki-Shua, were killed in the battle. When A Philistine arrow critically injured Saul, he requested that his armor-bearer kill him, but when he refused to do so, Saul, not wanting to be captured and tortured by the Philistines, deliberately fell on his own sword.

Mephibosheth was only five years old when his father Jonathan and his grandfather, Israel's former King (Saul), died during the Battle of Mount Gilboa. The Philistine army defeated the Israelites at this fateful battle. During that time, it was customary that when a ruler was defeated, his family would also be killed, eliminating any future claims to the throne by the ruler's family. However, God spared Mephibosheth's life as he survived the Philistine attack. When the news about Saul and Jonathan came from Jezreel, Mephibosheth's nurse hurriedly picked him up and fled to Gibeah. In her haste to save him, she fell and dropped Mephibosheth, injuring both his feet, and he became lame for the rest of his life. Losing his heritage and the ability to walk, Mephibosheth was reduced to nothing. He lived in a desolate place called Lo Debar, which means "land of nothing." Before Jonathan's death, King David and Jonathan had become close friends, like brothers. David and Jonathan had entered a covenant to protect and care for each other, including their families. David fulfilled his oath by extending grace and provision for Jonathan's son, Mephibosheth. When Mephibosheth was first located, he was ordered to go to King David. He was afraid, not knowing what David was going to do. When Mephibosheth approached David, he fell on his face and prostrated himself, humbly bowing. David's intentions were not to hurt Mephibosheth but to help him. David restored the profits from Mephibosheth's grandfather's wealth and all the land that belonged to Saul and invited Mephibosheth to permanently eat at the King's table as one of the King's sons. David also ordered his servants to work the land for Mephibosheth and take the harvest to him so that he would be provided for. King David did not allow a physical handicap, nor the initial shame brought upon Mephibosheth by his grandfather's sins to dictate his future.

This story is not just about going from rags to riches but an example of God's redemption and restoration. Though Mephibosheth lived in Lo Debar, God showed him mercy when David restored his inheritance, even with the accrued interest. Like in the case of Mephibosheth, God wants to do the same for us. No matter our economic status, our age, the color of our skin, handicapped, rejected, or hurt, God's doors are always opened to everyone. Like Mephibosheth, He will restore whatever was taken from us. So, what does God require from us? We need to start with humility before our God, asking for forgiveness and accepting Jesus Christ as our personal Savior and Lord that we might live in righteousness with Him. Therefore, we have the opportunity to become children of God and an heir to God and co-heirs with Jesus Christ (Romans 8: 17).

> *Now if we are children, then we are heirs —heirs of God and co-heirs with Christ, if indeed we share in his sufferings in order that we may also share in his glory.*
> *Romans 8:17 NIV*

- Cornealious Anderson

Cornealious Anderson III may not be a well-known name to many people, but his story shows how God can redeem anyone from a life of destruction.

Cornealious was known by his nickname Mike, and his story begins in Missouri when he was 23 years old. After robbing a Burger King employee at gunpoint, he was convicted of armed robbery, arrested, and sentenced to 13 years in prison. Fortunately, he was released on bail with instructions to await his orders to begin serving his time in prison. However, the orders never came through due to a strange clerical mix-up. I see this as the beginning of a second chance in life's journey to run from a life of crime into fellowship with God and servings others.

Realizing that he would not go to prison, he stayed away from a life of crime. Instead, he started a construction business (which expanded to three construction businesses) and volunteered to coach his son's youth football team. He was also in charge of the video operation at his local church. He settled down, married and divorced, then got married again and raised four children with his second wife.

Thirteen years later, when it was time to set Mike free from prison, the state realized that he had not served his time in prison. He simply wasn't there. As a result, he was arrested and made to serve nearly a year behind bars. Mike was well-liked within his community, and his story received international notoriety. Thousands of people signed a petition for his release. The judge reviewed his case and agreed that Mike was a changed man, and they released him, giving him credit with time served.

That was not the end of his story. Six months later, he was arrested; this time, he was charged for snatching a purse. He insisted he was innocent, but he was still charged with second-degree robbery. Mike informed the authorities that he was at a birthday party and was walking to his car at the time of the robbery. The robbery charges were dropped, and once again, he was declared a free man, and his name was cleared.

In this man's journey, we can see how God not only showed mercy but how he was redeemed from a life of destruction. When released the second time, he became teary-eyed as he walked out of the courthouse, thanking God. This speaks to me as a reminder of just how much each of our lives is valued in God's eyes.

Often, when we are young, we make mistakes, some small and some big whoppers. For the most part, I think people are honest but get themselves into situations that they don't know how to get out of it. Perhaps, that's why God chooses to give us not only a second chance but many chances. The Bible tells us not to judge but to show compassion towards each other. If someone is genuinely repentant and asks for forgiveness, we have a duty to work with them. This doesn't mean we are saying what they did was right. In fact, when circumstances require punishment, then people should be punished accordingly. But God does not stop there; He will show mercy, just as He did for Cornealious Anderson.

- The Prodigal Son

The story of the prodigal son is probably one of the most famous and touching Bible stories. It can be found in Luke 15:11-32. Before telling this story, Jesus told the story of the lost sheep, found in Luke 15:3-7. I believe that Jesus told these two stories together because He wanted to ensure that all of us would know just how important we are and how much He loves us. When we are lost, God does not give up on His children. He reels us in until we either repent and ask for forgiveness or, sadly, deny Him.

> *Then Jesus told them this parable:* [4] *"Suppose one of you has a hundred sheep and loses one of them. Doesn't he leave the ninety-nine in the open country and go after the lost sheep until he finds it?* [5] *And when he finds it, he joyfully puts it on his shoulders* [6] *and goes home. Then he calls his friends and neighbors together and says, 'Rejoice with me; I have found my lost sheep.'* [7] *I tell you that in the same way there will be more rejoicing in heaven over one sinner who repents than over ninety-nine righteous persons who do not need to repent.*
> *Luke 15:3-7 NIV*

Jesus told a story about a wealthy man that had two sons. The youngest son was foolish and asked his father to give him his inheritance. So, the father divided the estate into two and gave each son his portion. Even though the father loved his sons, the youngest departed to a far-off country, where he squandered his wealth frivolously. Then, there was a severe famine in that entire country, requiring the younger son to hire himself out to a farmer, who sent him to his fields to feed the pigs. Jews, in those days, considered pigs to be unclean, and the Law of Moses gave further instructions not to eat pork. Working with pigs was barely enough to eat himself; the younger son had reached a low point in his life. He finally came to his senses and decided that his father's hired servants ate and had food to spare while he was starving. He journeyed back home to tell his father that he had sinned against him and heaven, claiming that he was no longer worthy to be his son, but he wanted his father to make him like one of his servants. To his surprise, his father saw him coming from a distance, ran to him, kissed him, and threw his arms around him. His father was delighted that his son had come back, so he had the servants prepare a feast for him. The father further instructed the servants to put the best robe on him, give him a ring, and put sandals on his feet. The father said, *"For this son of mine was dead and is alive again; he was lost and is found"* (Luke 15:24 NIV).

God values our lives, and it pleases Him when His children return to Him. All of us fall short from time to time, but we must get up and go forward as we repent and ask for forgiveness. There is no greater love than the love of the Father, and He will receive us with open arms. Even after foolishly squandering his wealth, the prodigal son was redeemed by his father. Just like our heavenly Father, his father received him with open arms and a kiss. He was accepted without any changes to his status as a son. We, too, are sons and daughters and like Luke 15:7 and Luke 15:10 says, *"there is great joy in the presence of the angels of God in heaven when one sinner repents."* No sin is too great that God won't forgive when we come to our senses and repent.

> *"I tell you that in the same way there will be more rejoicing in heaven over one sinner who repents than over ninety-nine righteous persons who do not need to repent."*
>
> *Luke 15:7 NIV*
>
> *In the same way, I tell you, there is rejoicing in the presence of the angels of God over one sinner who repents."*
>
> *Luke 15:10 NIV*

Chapter 6

Walking in Someone Else's Shoes

The Bible is strict in saying that we are to walk on the path of righteousness, which can only be accomplished by following in Jesus's footsteps. He not only taught this but demonstrated it with His life. We are not to judge or be jealous of others, especially those blessed by God. Unfortunately, we see people with eyes that can only see the surface, and the outward appearance is not always a true picture of what the individual may be experiencing. One may display a smile on the outside and seem to be on top of the world, yet inwardly they are crying. If we knew the truth, we probably would be thankful we were not going through whatever challenges they may be facing. Let's look at the life of King David, a man after God's heart.

- King David:

King David's life was devoted to God, yet he often failed in his journey of life by committing serious sins, as recorded in the Old Testament. David, as described in Acts 13:22, is a man after God's own heart. God examines the heart of man, as He did with David, and found David to be a young man of integrity who put God first, trusting in Him. David trusted in the Word of God, and he put the will of God above his own. Nonetheless, David was not a perfect person. His failures and sins disqualified him, as it does us, the privilege of being perfect. No one is flawless or without sin. Our sinful nature causes us to keep falling short of God's glory (Romans 3:23 & Ecclesiastes 7:20). Seeking God's heart and willing to be righteous does not qualify anyone to be perfect. In fact, Jesus is the only one who walked on earth that is perfect and without sin (1 Peter 2:22).

> *Then they asked for a king, and God gave them Saul the son of Kish, a man of the tribe of Benjamin, for forty years. And when he had removed him, he raised up David to be their king, of whom he testified and said, I have found in David the son of*

> *Jesse a man after my heart, who will do all my will.'*
> *Acts 13:22 ESV*

> *For all have sinned and fall short of the glory of God.*
> *Romans 3:23 NIV*

> *Indeed, there is no one on earth who is righteous, no one who does what is right and never sins.*
> *Ecclesiastes 7:20 NIV*

> *"He (Jesus) committed no sin, and no deceit was found in his mouth."*
> *1 Peter 2:22 NIV*

David's reliance upon God was demonstrated when he was just a shepherd boy fighting against Goliath (1 Samuel 17:45). Standing toe to toe with this giant, David said, "…I come to you in the name of the LORD Almighty." I can say with confidence that I would not have even thought to volunteer to fight even a small warrior, much less a giant. David's high level of confidence came from knowing that he could rely on God's power and strength, which left no doubt in his mind that he would be victorious. We should all have the same level of confidence in our Savior and Lord. Unfortunately, most of us don't. You may ask, why? We struggle to have confidence in God that we allow doubt to creep into our minds, especially during hard times. We want instant gratification; that is, we want our prayers to be answered "now," but when our requests are not granted immediately, we start to panic. In these times, we need to reject those thoughts, knowing that God hears our prayers and He is working behind the scenes to help us. He loves us and wants only the best for us.

> *David said to the Philistine, "You come against me with sword and spear and javelin, but I come against you in the name of the LORD Almighty, the God of the armies of Israel, whom you have defied.*
> *1 Samuel 17:45 NIV*

I. David's accomplishments

As stated above, David's life was filled with many accomplishments and failures. First, let's take a look at some of his accomplishments:

- God anointed David:

God anointed David to be the king of Israel when he was just a boy. David was a shepherd boy from the little town of Bethlehem, and his job was to watch after his father's flock. As the youngest of eight sons, his father had overlooked him as someone who could be the next king. David's father was not aware that God had chosen David to be the next King of Israel. David followed the kingship of Saul, the first king of Israel. The Lord appointed David to be the leader of His people. The events that occurred during the time David awaited his tenure as king is summarized below:

The Lord directed Samuel (Samuel was the first of Israel's great prophets and the last of the judges) to meet with Jesse in his search for the new king (Jesse was the son of Ohed, Boaz and Ruth's grandson, a farmer, and sheep breeder in Bethlehem). At first, Jesse only presented his older sons, of which neither was chosen. Samuel knew that God had directed him to Jesse to find the next king, but since none of the older boys were chosen, Samuel asked Jesse if he had any other sons. Jesse replied, "yes." David was not the biggest nor the strongest of Jesse's sons, but God saw his heart and knew He could rely on David to obey and fulfill His will. David repeatedly declared his love of God's word in his Psalms. Samuel anointed David with oil in the presence of his brothers, and from that day on, the Spirit of the Lord came powerfully upon David (1 Samuel 16:13).

> *So, Samuel took the horn of oil and anointed him in the presence of his brothers, and from that day*

> *on the Spirit of the LORD came powerfully upon David.*
> *1 Samuel 16:13 NIV*

- David's Allegiance to God

David's allegiance to God kept him away from idolatry, the worship of idols. Unlike most of the forty-plus kings of Israel and Judah, including David's own Solomon, David did not fall into idolatry (1 Kings 11:4). In the Bible, there are over 40 verses that warn us against worshiping idols. Deuteronomy 6:13 and Luke 4:8 command us to only worship the Lord our God and only serve Him. I have heard several Christian speakers say that their allegiance was to God, and after studying the bible, I have come to understand that our hope, faith, and trust should be directed only to God Almighty (The Father, The Son, and The Holy Spirit) and no one else.

> *As Solomon grew old, his wives turned his heart after other gods, and his heart was not fully devoted to the LORD his God, as the heart of David his father had been.*
> *1 Kings 11:4 NIV*

> *You shall fear [only] the Lord your God; and you shall serve Him [with awe-filled reverence and profound respect] and swear [oaths] by His name [alone].*
> *Deuteronomy 6:13 Amplified[7]*

> *Jesus answered, "It is written: 'Worship the Lord your God and serve him only.'*
> *Luke 4:8 NIV*

- David Defeated Goliath:

As a boy, David killed Goliath, a fearsome Philistine giant and warrior. He trusted God while fighting this single battle. David won this victory, armed with courage, faith in God, and a sling with one smooth stone. He relied on God's mighty power to give him the wisdom and strength to conquer the giant. He understood that because of God's power and protection that he could always rely on Him. God had revealed this protection when he was a shepherd boy caring for the sheep when God delivered David from many perils, including the paws of lions and bears (1 Samuel 17:37, 40, 45, 47, and 50). The Bible is filled with many verses directing us to trust in the Lord. Jesus paid the price by tak-

---

[7] Source: https://bible.knowing-jesus.com/Deuteronomy/6/13

ing all of our iniquities upon Himself when He was crucified. When we seek the kingdom of God with our whole heart, soul, and mind, God gives us wisdom, peace, and protection. Psalm 91 reveals the many promises of God for those who take shelter in the Most High God.

> [37] *And David said, "The LORD who delivered me from the paw of the lion and from the paw of the bear will deliver me from the hand of this Philistine." And Saul said to David, "Go, and the LORD be with you!" ...* [40] *Then he took his staff in his hand and chose five smooth stones from the brook and put them in his shepherd's pouch. His sling was in his hand, and he approached the Philistine ...* [45] *Then David said to the Philistine, "You come to me with a sword and with a spear and with a javelin, but I come to you in the name of the LORD of hosts, the God of the armies of Israel, whom you have defied. This day the LORD will deliver you into my hand, and I will strike you down and cut off your head...*.[47] *For the battle is*

the LORD'S, and he will give you into our hand." ... ⁵⁰So David prevailed over the Philistine with a sling and with a stone, and struck the Philistine and killed him.

1 Samuel 17:37, 40, 45, 47, and 50 ESV

Psalm 91

Whoever dwells in the shelter of the Most High will rest in the shadow of the Almighty I will say of the LORD, "He is my refuge and my fortress, my God, in whom I trust." Surely, he will save you from the fowler's snare and from the deadly pestilence. He will cover you with his feathers, and under his wings you will find refuge; his faithfulness will be your shield and rampart. You will not fear the terror of night, nor the arrow that flies by day, nor the pestilence that stalks in the darkness, nor the plague that destroys at midday.

Life's Journey

A thousand may fall at your side, ten thousand at your right hand, but it will not come near you. You will only observe with your eyes and see the punishment of the wicked. If you say, "The LORD is my refuge," and you make the Most High your dwelling, no harm will overtake you; no disaster will come near your tent.

For he will command his angels concerning you to guard you in all your ways; they will lift you up in their hands, so that you will not strike your foot against a stone. You will tread on the lion and the cobra; you will trample the great lion and the serpent. "Because he loves me," says the LORD, "I will rescue him; I will protect him, for he acknowledges my name. He will call on me, and I will answer him; I will be with him in trouble, I will deliver him and honor him.

With long life I will satisfy him and show him my salvation."

- David the Lyrist:

As a shepherd boy, David worshiped God by playing his lyre while he was out tending the sheep. The Lord's favor was demonstrated when He promoted David from shepherd boy to ruler over all Israel. Before David's coronation, he worked as one of Kings Saul's servants. The king found favor in David. David played the lyre beautifully, so he was chosen to play for King Saul. King Saul repeatedly disobeyed the commands of the Lord, and he was not repentant, so God rejected him as king of Israel. When the spirit of the Lord departed from Saul, an evil spirit from the Lord tormented him. David was called to play his lyre during the night when King Saul suffered from nightmares which affected his mind and body. While David played the lyre, the melodious refrains calmed King Saul, so he felt better, and the evil spirits departed from him (1 Samuel 16:23).

> *Whenever the spirit from God came on Saul, David would take up his lyre and play. Then relief would come to Saul; he would feel better, and the evil spirit would leave him.*
> *1 Samuel 16:23 NIV*

Life's Journey

Growing up, I had nightmares of giant spiders that would scare me and wake me up. To conquer the nightmare, I learned that if I said the Lord's Prayer, I would go back to sleep, and the nightmares would go away. Praying the Lord's Prayer is one way of reaching to God for help because by saying this prayer, we are worshiping Him and honoring Him. But, in this story, King Saul's punishment manifested not only nightmares but an evil spirit that tormented him, affecting his body and mind. Thank God for giving him David and the relief King Saul felt when David played his lyre.

- David the Psalmist:

David was not only a lyrist, but he composed many of the Psalms found in the Old Testament of the Bible. He is accredited for writing 73 Psalms. Psalms 3-9, 11-32, 34-41, 51-65, 68-70, 86, 101, 103, 108-110, 122, 124, 131, 133, 138-145. His Psalms commemorate some events of his life as a musician, king, warrior, and shepherd. Here are just a few of the themes behind the Psalms, according to Got Questions:

1. <u>Psalm 3</u>: A Psalm of David, when he fled from Absalom, his son.
2. <u>Psalm 7</u>: A Shiggaion (see below for definition of Shiggaion) of David, which he

sang to the Lord concerning the words of Cush, a Benjaminite.

3. <u>Psalm 30</u>: A Psalm of David. A song at the dedication of the temple.
4. <u>Psalm 34</u>: Of David, when he changed his behavior before Abimelech so that he drove him out, and he went away.
5. <u>Psalm 51</u>: A Psalm of David, when Nathan the prophet went to him after he had gone to Bathsheba.
6. <u>Psalm 52</u>: A Maskil/Maschil (The definition of Maskil is provided below) of David, when <u>Doeg the Edomite</u> (A servant of King Saul) came and told Saul, "David has come to the house of Ahimelech."
7. <u>Psalm 54</u>: A Maskil of David, when the Ziphites went and told Saul, "Is not David hiding among us?"
8. <u>Psalm 56</u>: A Miktam of David, when the Philistines seized him in Gath.
9. <u>Psalm 57</u>: A Miktam of David, when he fled from Saul, in the cave.
10. <u>Psalm 59</u>: A Miktam of David, when Saul sent men to watch his house to kill him.
11. <u>Psalm 60</u>: A Miktam of David; for instruction; when he strove with Aram-naharaim and with Aram-zobah, and when Joab on his return struck down twelve thousand of Edom in the Valley of Salt.

12. Psalm 63: A Psalm of David, when he was in the wilderness of Judah.
13. Psalm 142: A Maskil of David, when he was in the cave. A Prayer.
14. David's psalms express a heart devoted to God. His music comforted King Saul, influenced his nation, and continues to change lives today.[8]

Below are a couple of definitions of words used above, *Shiggaion* and *Maskil*. Since I was not familiar with them, I looked them up for all of us.

The definition of Shiggaion:

> No one actually knows for sure what the Hebrew word *shiggaion* means in the title to Psalm 7, nor the plural of it ("*shigionoth*") in (Habakkuk 3:1). This being the case, there are several logical guesses as to the meaning.

> The words that follow in the title to Psalm 7, "which he sang," make it seem like it has something to do with a song. In Habakkuk 3:1, it says, "A prayer of Habakkuk the prophet upon *Shigionoth*." If you look at the end of Habakkuk 3:1, you will find the words "To the chief singer on my stringed instruments."

---
[8] https://www.gotquestions.org/Psalms-David.html

So, putting these together, perhaps we have a prayer that was sung. What kind of "prayer/song?" Let me quote some classic sources for definitions:

Smith's Bible Dictionary: perhaps a "wild, mournful ode."

Hitchcock Dictionary: a song of trouble or comfort

Easton's Bible Dictionary: denotes a lyrical poem composed under strong mental emotion; a song of impassioned imagination accompanied with suitable music; a dithyrambic ode (Dithyramb = 1: a usu. short poem in an inspired wild irregular strain 2: a statement or writing in an exalted or enthusiastic vein – Webster's Dictionary)

International Standard Bible Encyclopedia: Derived from a verb meaning "to wander," it is generally taken to mean a dithyramb or rhapsody

Holman's Bible Dictionary: Suggested translations include "frenzied" or "emotional."

The NKJV Bible replaces the word "*shiggaion*" with the word "meditation."

> These words are used nowhere else in the Old Testament. Again, their meaning is uncertain.[9]

The definition of *Maskil* according to Got Questions.org.

> *Maskil* is a term of uncertain meaning found in the book of Psalms. Most Bible translations suggest that *maskil* is a literary or musical term. Most likely, it relates to the purpose of specific psalms or how they were performed or recited.[10]

- David Conquered Jerusalem:

The Lord Almighty was with King David when he recaptured Jerusalem from the Jebusites. These were enemies that seemed too strong to defeat because no other tribe could overtake them. David was heavily armed, and he took the Jebusite guards by surprise by climbing up the shaft and tunnel used to haul water from outside the city wall. David captured the fortress of Zion and the City of David. He designated Jerusalem as the capital of Israel (2 Samuel 5:6-10).

---

[9] https://jesusalive.cc/shiggaion-meaning-psalm-seven/ by Steve Shirley
[10] https://www.gotquestions.org/maskil.html

> *The king and his men marched to Jerusalem to attack the Jebusites, who lived there. The Jebusites said to David, "You will not get in here; even the blind and the lame can ward you off." They thought, "David cannot get in here." Nevertheless, David captured the fortress of Zion —which is the City of David. On that day David had said, "Anyone who conquers the Jebusites will have to use the water shaft to reach those 'lame and blind' who are David's enemies." That is why they say, "The 'blind and lame' will not enter the palace."*
>
> *David then took up residence in the fortress and called it the City of David. He built up the area around it, from the terraces inward. And he became more and more powerful, because the LORD God Almighty was with him.*
>
> *2 Samuel 5:6-10 NIV*

The enemy thought that no one could conquer them, but God gave David wisdom, and David captured the fortress. At this point, I would say, "Never say never," for, with God, all things are possible when we follow His instructions.

- The Ark of the Covenant:

Because of the sins of David, a time of judgment was inflicted upon Israel. At the same time, God revealed the place for his future Temple to be built. Before the Temple was built, David temporarily positioned the Ark of the Covenant in a tent in Jerusalem (2 Sam. 6:16-17). David planned and supplied the resources to build the Temple. Because of David's enthusiasm, he did all he could to make sure the Temple would be magnificently built. Even though he was not allowed to build it himself (God had appointed his son Solomon to build it), he provided stones, bronze, and cedar logs, doing all he could before he died (1 Chronicles 22:1-10 NIV).

> *As the ark of the LORD was entering the City of David, they brought the ark of the LORD and set it in its place inside the tent that David had pitched for it, and David sacrificed burnt offerings and fellowship offerings before the LORD.*
> *2 Samuel 6:16-17 NIV*

Then David said, "The house of the LORD God is to be here, and also the altar of burnt offering for Israel." So, David gave orders to assemble the foreigners residing in Israel, and from among them he appointed stonecutters to prepare dressed stone for building the house of God. He provided a large amount of iron to make nails for the doors of the gateways and for the fittings, and more bronze than could be weighed. He also provided more cedar logs than could be counted, for the Sidonians and Tyrians had brought large numbers of them to David.

David said, "My son Solomon is young and inexperienced, and the house to be built for the LORD should be of great magnificence and fame and splendor in the sight of all the nations. Therefore, I will make preparations for it." So, David made extensive preparations before his death.

Then he called for his son Solomon and charged him to build a house

> *for the LORD, the God of Israel. David said to Solomon: "My son, I had it in my heart to build a house for the Name of the LORD my God. But this word of the LORD came to me: 'You have shed much blood and have fought many wars. You are not to build a house for my Name, because you have shed much blood on the earth in my sight. But you will have a son who will be a man of peace and rest, and I will give him rest from all his enemies on every side. His name will be Solomon, and I will grant Israel peace and quiet during his reign. He is the one who will build a house for my Name. He will be my son, and I will be his father. And I will establish the throne of his kingdom over Israel forever.'*
>
> *1 Chronicles 22:1-10 NIV*

As you can see from the previous scripture, God did not allow David to build the Temple because he was a man of war and had shed too much blood. Solomon, his son, was a man of peace and was chosen by God to build it instead. The ark of the covenant of the Lord was placed in the inner sanctuary within the temple.

When God says, "no," there is always a reason. In David's case, he wanted to build the Temple, but God said no. At times, when God says no to us, I believe that He is either saving us from something we do not foresee, sparing us from tragedy, or perhaps the timing is off, and we just need to wait. Or, in David's case, God has chosen someone else to 'build the temple,' so to speak.

- Ministering before the Ark of the Lord:

David was diligent in ensuring that the Ark was permanently established, allowing continuous worship of God in Jerusalem. David delegated Levites to minister before the Ark, and each was assigned specific duties. 1 Chronicles 16:4-6 gives detailed instructions for ministering before the Ark. The Levites were to minister in an attitude of worship, thanksgiving and praise, playing the lyres and harps, and blowing the trumpets regularly before the Ark.

> *He appointed some of the Levites to minister before the ark of the LORD, to extol, thank, and praise the LORD, the God of Israel: Asaph was the chief, and next to*

> *him in rank were Zechariah, then Jaaziel, Shemiramoth, Jehiel, Mattithiah, Eliab, Benaiah, Obed-Edom and Jeiel. They were to play the lyres and harps, Asaph was to sound the cymbals, and Benaiah and Jahaziel the priests were to blow the trumpets regularly before the ark of the covenant of God.*
> *1 Chronicles 16:4-6 NIV*

Assigning different individuals to perform the many tasks in watching over the Ark reminds me that we are individually needed and can be used to spread the Good News of Jesus Christ. God gives us talents to use for ministering either in the church or elsewhere. There are many jobs within the church, and a pastor simply cannot do them all by himself. Don't forget to volunteer. The church is like the body; the eye sees but cannot hold on to anything as that is the duty of the hand. Likewise, all of us have talents and are part of the body that is needed to keep the doors of the church open to minister to others.

- God's covenant with David:

God's covenant with David came with a promise to establish David on an everlasting throne. God gave David promises not only while he was alive but also after he died.

1. While David was alive:
According to 2 Samuel 7:9-10, God gave David a great name and God provided a place for His people, Israel. In 2 Samuel 7:11, God gave David rest from all his enemies.

> *I have been with you wherever you have gone, and I have cut off all your enemies from before you. Now I will make your name great, like the names of the greatest men on earth. And I will provide a place for my people Israel and will plant them so that they can have a home of their own and no longer be disturbed.*
> *2 Samuel 7:9-10 NIV*

> *…I will also give you rest from all your enemies.*
> *2 Samuel 7:11 NIV*

2. Promises Made after David Dies:
After David's death, the Lord accomplished what He promised David, raising and caring for his son, Solomon, and establishing an everlast-

ing kingdom through Jesus Christ (2 Samuel 7:12-16).

Bible-Studys.org states it this way:

(1) A son to sit on his national throne, who the Lord would oversee as a father with necessary chastening, discipline, and mercy (Solomon).
And
(2) A Son who would rule a kingdom that will be established forever (Messiah).[11]

> *When your days are over and you rest with your ancestors, I will raise up your offspring to succeed you, your own flesh and blood, and I will establish his kingdom. He is the one who will build a house for my Name, and I will establish the throne of his kingdom forever. I will be his father, and he will be my son. When he does wrong, I will punish him with a rod wielded by men, with floggings inflicted by human hands. But my love will never be*

---

[11] https://bible-studys.org/Bible%20Books/2%20Samuel/2%20Samuel%20Chapter%207.html

> *taken away from him, as I took it away from Saul, whom I removed from before you. Your house and your kingdom will endure forever before me; your throne will be established forever.*
> *2 Samuel 7:12-16 NIV*

- David's Confidence Was in God, not with Self:

David trusted God and put his confidence in God's hands:
David demonstrated confidence, which resulted from the many miracles God performed in front of him, even while he was a young boy. God used David's confidence to develop him into a mighty warrior and empire builder. David understood that his strength and power were not of his own doing but because of God's support in his life. David was a soldier with a vision, and he was successful throughout the many military battles he fought.

As we can see, David was a strong warrior but realized that his strength did not come from within but from his Lord, God Almighty. He was not shy to proclaim his allegiance to God.

II. List of Some of David's Failures.

It is interesting to think that many of David's choices should have resulted in his dethroning or banishment from Israel. He could have been executed for the murder of Bathsheba's husband, Uriah the Hittite. Even worse, he could have been condemned to hell to suffer eternal punishment, but because of God's mercy and grace, he was forgiven, allowing him to remain in power. God bestowed favor upon David because he genuinely repented and sought after God. God generously extends His mercy and grace (Mercy is not getting what we deserve, and grace is receiving what we do not deserve). In Galatians 6:7, we are reminded that "what we sow we will reap." Throughout the Bible, David showed mercy towards others. For example, David showed mercy towards Jonathan's son, Mephibosheth, by restoring what belonged to him and allowing him to eat at the King's table like one of his own sons.

> *Do not be deceived: God cannot be mocked. A man reaps what he sows.*
>
> *Galatians 6:7 NIV*

- Adultery and Murder:

David committed the sin of adultery with Uriah the Hittite's wife, Bathsheba, resulting in the birth of a son, and she sent word to inform David that she was pregnant with his baby. See 2 Samuel 11:1-5.

> *One evening David got up from his bed and walked around on the roof of the palace. From the roof he saw a woman bathing. The woman was very beautiful, and David sent someone to find out about her. The man said, "She is Bathsheba, the daughter of Eliam and the wife of Uriah the Hittite." Then David sent messengers to get her. She came to him, and he slept with her. (Now she was purifying herself from her monthly uncleanness.) Then she went back home. The woman conceived and sent word to David, saying, "I am pregnant."*
> *2 Samuel 11:1-5 NIV*

When David found out that Bathsheba was pregnant with his child, he entered into a spiral of deception to hide his sin. He sent for Uriah, hoping he would sleep with his wife and thus believe that the child was his. But Uriah did not sleep with his wife because he was concerned for his fellow warriors who were engaged in battle for their country. In 2 Samuel 11:11, Uriah said to David, "The ark and Israel and Judah are staying in tents, and my commander Joab and my lord's men are camped in the open country. How could I go to my house to eat and drink and make love to my wife? As surely as you live, I will not do such a thing!" David became desperate and launched a plan to have Uriah eliminated (2 Samuel 11:14-15). He commanded Joab, in a letter, to put Uriah out in front, where the severest fighting took place. Even though David did not directly strike Uriah, his death was in his hands. David was the commander behind the scheme, which displeased the Lord (2 Samuel 11:26-27).

> *In the morning David wrote a letter to Joab and sent it with Uriah. In it he wrote, "Put Uriah out in front where the fighting is fiercest. Then withdraw from him so he will be struck down and die."*
> *2 Samuel 11:14-15 NIV*

Upon receiving the news that Bathsheba's husband had been killed, she mourned for him. David then took her to his house, and she became his wife. Soon after, their son was born (2 Samuel 11:26-27).

> *When Uriah's wife heard that her husband was dead, she mourned for him. After the time of mourning was over, David had her brought to his house, and she became his wife and bore him a son. But the thing David had done displeased the LORD.*
> *2 Samuel 11:26-27 NIV*

Often, when we sin, we will try to hide what we have done. This can cause a chain reaction, first trying to deceive, followed by lies, until we have strayed very far from the path of truth. In this case, first David had an affair, then he tried to cover it up by bringing her husband home to sleep with her. When that did not work, he became desperate and had Uriah killed. Can you see the slippery slope of deceptions David carried out? If we make a mistake or are weak and fall short, we should always speak the truth immediately and not allow sin to entangle us, leading us into more sin. We are to repent from our sins with a sincere heart and ask God for forgiveness. God is always ready to forgive us, and He will receive us with open arms.

You may ask, what the progression of sin is? It starts with a thought. When we first get a sinful thought, we are to instantly dismiss the thought before giving birth to the actual sin. The sequence of birthing a sin starts when after a wrongful thought occurs, we act on it and are absorbed in it and soon become unable to walk away from it on our own. God foresaw our weakness and gave us a way out. We can be overcomers with God's help through Jesus Christ. Jesus paid the price while on the cross. He took our sins upon Himself so that we could overcome the challenges of life that try to take us down. Jesus said, *"By my stripes you are healed"* (1 Peter 2:24). Him taking on our sins allows us to die to sin no more and live righteously.

> *"He himself bore our sins" in his body on the cross, so that we might die to sins and live for righteousness; "by his wounds you have been healed."*
>
> *1 Peter 2:25 NIV*

- David's Son's Demise:

As we see in 2 Samuel 11:27, God was not pleased with David because he not only lusted with his eyes, but he committed adultery with Bathsheba (note, he did not rape her, as she consented). Then David willfully planned the death of Uriah. Even though he did not kill him himself, he was responsible for taking Uriah's life. After a period of mourning, he took Bathsheba as his wife. In 2 Samuel 12:15, the Lord struck the child, and he became ill and died on the seventh day. When we sin against God, be sure there are consequences that can cause lifelong regrets, as in this case, the death of a child.

> *After Nathan had gone home, the LORD struck the child that Uriah's wife had borne to David, and he became ill. David pleaded with God for the child. He fasted and spent the nights lying in sackcloth on the ground. The elders of his household stood beside him to get him up from the ground, but he refused, and he would not eat any food with them. On the seventh day the child died.*
> *2 Samuel 12:15-18 NIV*

- Unauthorized Census and a Plague:

When the anger of the Lord burned against Israel, Satan rose and incited David to take a census of the available fighting men in Israel, which is against God's will. David also ignored the advice of Joab, the army commander, by taking the census (2 Samuel 24:4). David instructed Joab to enroll the fighting men of Israel so that he would be advised as to how many men he had at his disposal (2 Samuel 24:2). This displeased the Lord. David pleaded for mercy, but the Lord responded by giving David three options for his punishment. The options were:

1) Three years of famine in the land.
2) Three months of fleeing from his enemies.
3) Three days of plague in the land.

David was in distress, and he did not want to be captured or, as the scripture said it, "to fall into human hands." Thus, the Lord sent a plague on Israel, killing seventy thousand people from Dan to Beersheba (2 Samuel 24:15).

> *The king's word, however, overruled Joab and the army commanders; so, they left the presence of the king to enroll the fighting men of Israel.*
>
> 2 Samuel 24:4 NIV

> *So, the king said to Joab and the army commanders with him, "Go throughout the tribes of Israel from Dan to Beersheba and enroll the fighting men, so that I may know how many there are."*
>
> 2 Samuel 24:2 NIV

> *"Go and tell David, 'This is what the LORD says: I am giving you*

> *three options. Choose one of them for me to carry out against you.'"* So, Gad went to David and said to him, "Shall there come on you three years of famine in your land? Or three months of fleeing from your enemies while they pursue you? Or three days of plague in your land? Now then, think it over and decide how I should answer the one who sent me."
>
> *2 Samuel 24:12-13 NIV*

> *So, the LORD sent a plague on Israel from that morning until the end of the time designated, and seventy thousand of the people from Dan to Beersheba died.*
> *2 Samuel 24:15 NIV*

As we have seen, sin comes with consequences; in this case, God spared David's life, but He did not escape the punishment. At times, God will show His mercy and grace for those who truly repent and ask for forgiveness, allowing us to forego the consequences we deserve. This doesn't mean that God has favorites; we simply don't see the divine plans of God nor what is required for each of us to remain on the path of righteousness. We have

Life's Journey

to ask ourselves, "did we sin because we thought we were above reproach, did we make a mistake, or is God using this for His glory?" We need to keep our eyes on God so that we do not fail in our walk with Him. We must follow God's will for our lives.

- David's Life Summary:

David's life can be described as one in deep despair, resulting from the many war-like, near-death experiences. Throughout David's life, he patiently waited upon God, believing that God would answer him. God did as He promised, rescuing David from his enemies and leading him to shelter. David described times of devastation as being in a pit of destruction and miry clay. When I think of this verse, a visual that comes to mind is the idea of quicksand (Okay, this only happens in action movies and usually in the jungle). The sand devours its victim when they fall into the pit. The person that falls into it starts to sink, and the more they struggle, the faster they go down into the muck. The only way to be saved is if someone pulls the sinking person out (Psalm 40:2 ESV).

> He drew me up from the pit of destruction, out of the miry bog, and set my feet upon a rock, making my steps secure.
> Psalm 40:2 ESV

When you think about how much David accomplished throughout his journey of life, you may say, "wow," he has done so much, and he should be thankful for all of his success stories. After all, he was a mighty warrior, an accomplished lyrist, palmist, leader, and a man after God's own heart. But what lessons did he have to learn when he was disobedient to the will of God? There were consequences for his actions, even when he confessed his sins and repented. In some of his actions, he tried to fool himself and others by hiding what he did, but be assured; no one can hide from God. Let's think about the consequence of David's adulterous act with Bathsheba. One foolish choice led to the murder of Bathsheba's husband, Uriah the Hittite, resulting in the death of David and Bathsheba's son. The repercussions not only haunted him and his family immediately but throughout the rest of their lives.

It is only with the grace of God that one can deal with such remorse. Our minds are powerful, and hanging onto the past can be devastating. Yet, God will always carry us and help us move forward when we turn to Him for forgiveness.

- Jerry Givens

Jerry Givens worked in Virginia's department of correction as a state-sanctioned executioner. He was responsible for putting inmates to death, but he sincerely regrets it, and now he campaigns to end capital punishment.

Givens' career with the Commonwealth of Virginia, department of corrections, lasted for 25 years, although his time as the state-sanctioned professional executioner lasted for 17 years (from 1982 - 1999). As an executioner, he administered and methodically carried out the killing of 62 people. The executions were done with either lethal injection or electrocution. This bothered him so much that he swore himself to secrecy, not telling his family or anyone else what he was doing. When Jerry took the job as an executioner, there wasn't anyone on death row, and he did not realize that he would eventually have to put people to death. When asked what the biggest mistake he had made while working, he responded, "taking the job of executioner."

While he worked as an executioner, he often thought of how he could help prevent children from walking down the path of crime, especially the path that would lead to death row. He gave tours to kids, letting them sit in the chair and telling them that they needed to get an education so they will not end up on death row. This strategy seemed to have positive results, as he would later receive letters of thanks from some of the children. It puzzled him that so much money was spent on executing these people rather than preventing crime by educating people.

As a Christian, Givens prayed with many of the condemned men before they were to be executed. He realized that it would be the last chance he would get to lead them to Jesus Christ. He would inform them that this was their last chance to repent and seek God's forgiveness. Like God, he did not want anyone to be condemned and to wake up in the pit of hell. Once a person dies, not having accepted Jesus Christ as their Savior and Lord, they are immediately separated from God and sent to hell where the devil, his demons, and wicked people are eternally punished. On the other hand, Believers will wake up in heaven in eternal glory once they have taken their last breath.

One day, Givens was wrongly convicted and sentenced to 57 months in a federal institution. He was accused of laundering money and for committing perjury over his supposed role in buying cars for a friend. This opened his eyes, or as he says, "God stepped in and said enough is enough." He realized that the system was flawed because he, himself, did not get a fair trial, and he wondered how many people were executed because they too, did not get a fair trial.

Givens, now an outspoken advocate, campaigns against capital punishment, that is, the abolition of the death penalty. He is the author of the book, <u>Another Day Not Promised</u>, an active member of Cedar Street Church in Richmond, and a truck driver. From 2009 until 2015, he was on the board of Virginians for Alternatives to the Death Penalty (VADP).

Givens said he would not have picked this job had he realized what it entailed. Taking the life of another is not an easy task. It makes it hard to go home and live a normal life. This job leaves people broken, as they witness another human-being being executed and mentally traumatized, often impacting the employee for the rest of their lives. It is a wrenching way to live. Additionally, some of the effects these prison executioners face are post-traumatic stress disorder (PTSD), nightmares, depression, sleeplessness, flashbacks, and cold sweats. A secondary trauma executioner can experience suicide, mental and physical health problems, and psychological trauma.

When Givens realized that capital punishment went against the Word of God, he decided that he needed to make this message more widely known. With direction from God, his experience as a sanctioned killer allowed the door to be opened for him to advocate against the death penalty and stop the death of innocent people in a broken court system.

The story of Jerry Givens reminds me that God uses every situation to promote his divine will. Had Givens realized what this job entailed and just how many lives would have been taken, he would not have accepted it. Yet, God took Jerry's faith as an opportunity to give inmates one last chance to accept Jesus before they were executed and to use Givens to advocate for the end of the death penalty, which I believe is in opposition to the Word of God.

Information was taken from:
https://www.theguardian.com/commentisfree/2013/nov/21/death-penalty-former-executioner-jerry-givens

https://www.psychologytoday.com/us/blog/talking-about-trauma/201810/prison-executioners-face-job-related-trauma

http://mtabolitionco.org/issues/secondary-trauma/

- ## Eric Liddell

Eric Liddell is well known for winning the 1924 Olympic 400-meter race, even though he was not expected to win. He refused to run the 100-meter race, even though he was among the fastest runners because it was scheduled to take place on a Sunday. Liddell refused to run on Sundays because it went against his religious beliefs.

Born in 1902, Eric Liddell's family was serving as missionaries in China. While they were on furlough, he was enrolled in a missionary boarding school. His call to sports as an athlete began in rugby and track. While in college, where he earned a Bachelor in Science, he began to run the 100 meters.

Liddell was given the honor of running in the 1924 Olympics 100 meters, competing for England. He was among the fastest runners in the world and had won that race many times. However, once he realized that the run would be on a Sunday, he refused to run to keep the Sunday sabbath, a day dedicated to the Lord and a day for rest. This was met with criticism; Scotland even called him a traitor. His coach put him in the 400-meter race because it would take place on a different day. Even though he was not expected to win, Liddell won the race, breaking the world record, by running it in 47.6 seconds.

As a Christian, Liddell's fame gave him the opportunity to share his beliefs, the Gospel of Jesus Christ with many people while in England. When World War II broke out, he returned to China to serve as a missionary, teaching Anglo Chinese, Chemistry, and coaching track and rugby. In addition, he taught Sunday school classes at the local church. During this time, all non-residents were incarcerated in Japanese prison camps. The conditions of these camps were deplorable, as disease spread and the inmates were starving, receiving only one meal per day, bread, and a bowl of soup. As one can imagine, the inmates were in battling despair. As the saying goes, they could not see the light at the end of the tunnel. Liddell was the one person that encouraged the prisoners. He helped people by teaching them, tutoring them, and keeping their hope alive.

Eric Liddell died in 1945 at the age of 46 when he became ill and was admitted to a hospital, where he was diagnosed with a brain tumor. When the news spread about his death, the children in the camp were distraught because he was like family to them. Liddell's life was not an easy road, yet he focused on serving the Lord. The prisoners were released just six months after his death.

Information for this story came from:
https://missionsbox.org/missionary-bio/eric-liddell/

Life's Journey

- Bethany Hamilton

I wouldn't classify Bethany Meilani Hamilton-Dirks as weak, but she easily could have been devastated by her circumstances and given up her dreams without her faith in Jesus Christ. At the National Prayer Breakfast, she stated that it was her faith that gave her the strength needed to move forward (see below for the article from Christian Post). Her life is an inspiring story of courage and determination to achieve her surfing goals, despite a near-deadly encounter with a vicious shark.

> "I felt as though I had lost more than just my arm," said Hamilton. "I thought that my hopes and dreams to become a pro-surfer and adventure the world were stripped away, but the faith I had in Jesus Christ gave me the strength to comprehend and lean on Him for understanding, even as a young girl."[12]

---

[12] https://www.christianpost.com/news/soul-surfer-bethany-hamilton-says-faith-in-jesus-christ-gives-her-strength-to-overcome-lifes-adversities-at-national-prayer-breakfast.html

Bethany Meilani Hamilton was born in Lihue, Kauai, in Hawaii, on February 8, 1990. She is the youngest of three siblings. Her brothers are Noah and Tim Hamilton. Her parent's names are Tom and Cheri, and they are Christians. Bethany was raised in a surfing family and thus could take command of the waves at an early age.

Her career began when she was only eight years old when she first started competitive surfing. However, in 2003, at the age of 13, her career was seemingly derailed when she was met with what could have been an end to her hopes and dreams. A vicious 14-foot tiger shark attacked her and bit off her left arm. Accepting the challenge handed to her with strong faith, determined spirit, a positive attitude, and the encouragement of her family, she went back to the ocean on her surfboard just one month later. Two years later, she won first place in the Explore Woman's Division of the NSSA National Championships.[13]

Today, Hamilton is a professional surfer, inspirational author, and public speaker.

---

[13] https://www.beliefnet.com/entertainment/sports/galleries/5-inspiring-athletes-who-overcame-disabilities.aspx

Here is just a glimpse of her encouraging words taken from *Surfer Today*:

> *Be a Light to God and the whole world.*
>
> *Being able to turn to Jesus after the shark attack kept me alive.*
>
> *Being creative on the waves is challenging, but we each create art in our own way.*
>
> *Being present means living your actual life, accepting it for what it is, and making the absolute most of it. Cut out the constant barrage of distractions so you can be truly present with the people and things that matter most.*[14]

Hamilton, now a heroic role model, also stated at the National Prayer Breakfast that losing her arm, which seems like a physical setback, helped her realize the greater purpose she had in her ministry outside of surfing to help others overcome adversity and encourage them never to give up hope.

---

[14] https://www.surfertoday.com/surfing/the-inspirational-quotes-by-bethany-hamilton

There is hope because of the love that Jesus has for everyone and how He gave up His life for us. In addition, God showers His children with His grace, mercy, peace, and love, unlike what the world offers. When something dreadful happens to us, we need to turn it into an opportunity to do something great that can help others, thus taking the focus off our own hardships. Also, in these difficult times, it is a great opportunity to stop and see just how much God loves us as He carries us through these times. He will bless us with unforeseen opportunities and accomplishments as He did for Hamilton.

Chapter 7

From Atheism to Christianity

Continuing with the theme that God can use every one of us to accomplish His plan and bring anyone to saving grace, let us look into three unlikely converts. C. S. Lewis, John Gilmour, and Phil Hensley self-proclaimed atheists, eventually turned to God and Jesus Christ as their Savior and Lord, proving that even the hardest of hearts can be turned and proclaimed truths of the Bible.

When I think of Atheism, I think of people who deny or do not believe in any God or spiritual being and reject all religious beliefs. The definition, according to duckduckgo.com, is as follows:

a•the•ism ā′thē-ĭz″əm

- *n.*
    Disbelief in or denial of the existence of God or gods.

- *n.*
  The doctrine that there is no God; denial of the existence of God.

- *n.*
  The denial of theism, that is, of the doctrine that the great first cause is a supreme, intelligent, righteous person.[15]

---

[15] https://duckduckgo.com/?q=atheism+definition+religion&t=osx&ia=definition

- C.S. Lewis

Clive Staples 'Jack' Lewis (1898-1963) was a twentieth-century novelist from Belfast, Ireland. He was a well-known author of more than 30 books. Additionally, he was a scholar, theologian, and well-recognized Christian author. While he started out as a noted atheist, in 1929, he abandoned atheism and converted to theism. In September 1931, he converted specifically to Christianity (cslewis.com). The following information was also taken from cslewis.com:

> Lewis wrote more than thirty books, allowing him to reach a vast audience, and his works continue to attract thousands of new readers every year. C. S. Lewis's most distinguished and popular accomplishments include *Mere Christianity*, *Out of the Silent Planet*, *The Great Divorce*, *The Screwtape Letters*, and the universally acknowledged classics in *The Chronicles of Narnia*. To date, the Narnia books have sold over 100 million copies and

have been transformed into three major motion pictures.[16]

C. S. Lewis was raised as a Christian. His family attended the Church of Ireland, but while he was a teenager, he rejected his faith, and at the age of 15, he declared himself to be an atheist. He said he did not believe in religion because of the lack of proof for it. Lewis took a long time before he changed his mind.

Conversion is a unique experience for everyone. Some, like Lewis, take many years, while others, like Saul (who later became the apostle and Paul), are immediate. Saul's conversion took place while traveling on Damascus Road. On this journey, he carried a letter from the temple's high priest in Jerusalem, permitting him to arrest anyone who associated and/or followed Jesus. Saul was known to be a persecutor of Jesus' followers. God appeared and spoke to Saul while on the road to Damascus. Saul immediately ceased to persecute Christians and became a follower of Jesus. This story is found in Acts 26:12-16.

> *"On one of these journeys I was going to Damascus with the authority and commission of the chief*

---

[16] https://www.cslewis.com/us/about-cs-lewis/

> *priests. About noon, King Agrippa, as I was on the road, I saw a light from heaven, brighter than the sun, blazing around me and my companions. We all fell to the ground, and I heard a voice saying to me in Aramaic, 'Saul, Saul, why do you persecute me? It is hard for you to kick against the goads.'*
>
> *"Then I asked, 'Who are you, Lord?'*
> *'I am Jesus, whom you are persecuting,' the Lord replied. 'Now get up and stand on your feet. I have appeared to you to appoint you as a servant and as a witness of what you have seen and will see of me."*
> *Acts 26:12-16 NIV*

Lewis was an atheist for about fifteen years before his conversion back to Christianity. He credited his conversion to his circle of friends. Over shared common interests, they slowly whittled away at his objections to Christianity. He was particularly influenced by a colleague named JRR Tolkien and a close circle of Christian friends. This reminds me of a saying, "It takes a village to raise a child." Sometimes, God uses the influence of multiple people to inspire and encourage a single person as they wrestle with questions and their beliefs about Jesus Christ.

The life of C.S. Lewis reminds me that God honors the prayers of parents, grandparents, and/or other family members and friends when a child is raised in faith. The promise states that "when children are raised in faith, even when they grow old, they will not depart from it" (Proverbs 22:6). Godly influences, either by action or word, are very powerful; that is why we must train our children, especially when they are little.

> *Train up a child in the way he should go, and even when he is old, he will not depart from it*
> *Proverbs 22:6 ASV*

The moral of the story is, if you think you are one of the worst offenders, such as an atheist, be rest assured, it's not too late to turn to God through Jesus Christ. He waits with open arms to receive you into the Kingdom of God, as He did with C.S. Lewis, and not just now, but through eternity.

• John Gilmour

John Gilmour was born Scottish but migrated early on to Australia, where he became a successful lawyer, barrister, and eventually, a Federal Court judge. He married his sweetheart, Marcia, but that relationship encountered challenges as he walked out on her and his family. As a child, he lived in a small village, attending school and church. His father was an elder in the church, and he worked on a farm. At the age of 12, Gilmour was given the option of whether or not he would attend church., He chose to stop going altogether. While he was attending the university, studying law, he became cynical towards Christianity and despised Christians.

During his separation from his wife, Gilmour and a friend who was also alone due to a failed marriage shared a flat (apartment) in Australia. Though they pretended to be happy, Gilmour knew deep down in his heart that he was unhappy.

John's friend became a Christian and professed that Jesus had changed his life. But John was still cynical and hostile towards Christianity and did not want anything to do with Jesus or Christian beliefs. To get his friend off his back, John agreed to go to church, and if nothing happened, his friend was to never speak to him about Jesus.

This is where I say God has a sense of humor. The following Sunday, they went to church, and guess who was there? That's right, his wife, who was also a non-believer. The night before, she passed the church, saw the neon-lit cross, and decided to visit the church. She missed the service she had intended to go to and ended up at the same service that her husband was at. The sermon for the day was about Jonah. God called Jonah to go to Nineveh to save the wicked people, but he ran the opposite way and ended up in the belly of a big fish. God saved Jonah after he repented, and Jonah did go to Nineveh, where the people also repented and were saved. This story got Mr. Gilmour thinking about his life, and by the end of the service, he realized that there was a God and that God loved him.

With the new change in their lives, John and Marcia decided to give their marriage a second chance. John said that this unexpected experience and witnessing how his wife's life had changed led him to become a Christian too. His faith has remained strong, believing that God continues to work in and through him. He compared this change to a move from darkness to light.

Another life changed from a non-believer to passionately following Jesus Christ should give us hope that God does not give up on us. In fact, His love for humanity is above what we can comprehend. God wants fellowship with us now and through eternity.

John Gilmour passed away in February 2021

Information obtained from - https://www.is-there-a-god.info/life/gilmour/

- **Phil Hemsley**

Unlike the previous examples, Phil Hemsley was not raised in a Christian environment and believed that science had refuted the idea that there was a God. He sided with the ideas of atheism or at least agnosticism. In fact, he thought that Christianity was merely a crutch for the weak. His conversion to Christianity was slow. He was 40 before he would even consider the possibility of its validity.

With a closed mind towards Christianity, Phil would challenge those that approached him about the subject. However, one day, he joined in on a discussion around his kitchen table on the topic of "Why people aren't attracted to the church." Hemsley's theory was challenged by one of his Christian friends, to the point that he felt he needed to at least accept the possibility that they could be correct because he could see the peace his friends had in their belief.

This same friend lent him the book, Beyond Belief, which was an introduction to Christianity. Subsequently, through his own research to prove that Christianity was a myth and after thinking about his outlook on life, he decided to read the gospels. He realized that science did not prove nor disprove God. His research continued to leave him with many questions, but he concluded that science and God could co-exist.

Jesus' story of the crucifixion stirred something in Hemsley. Knowing that this man, Jesus, allowed himself to be nailed on a cross and learning about his teachings, not to judge others and forgive, he felt he should study Christianity with an open mind. After studying Jesus' life, he concluded that the Bible stories were scientifically possible. Thus, he decided to give God a chance. To summarize his conversion experience, he said that he felt an overwhelming experience of 'coming home and felt a weight lifted off him. Once, I felt that same weight lifted off my shoulders, and I can say that it gave me peace that I had never felt before. When the decision to embrace God is made, He may reveal to you His approval in this way. As a Christian, Hemsley learned that there is a creator, and Jesus is crucial for faith and eternal salvation.

Knowing that someone challenged the beliefs of Christianity and took time to defend them, using science, and then came to the conclusion that Jesus is the only mediator to God should give us hope and authenticate the truths we read in the Bible.

The above was taken from: https://www.is-there-a-god.info/life/phemsley/

Chapter 8

God Uses Ordinary People

- Chuck Norris

Chuck Norris was born Carlos Ray Norris, Jr. in Ryan, Oklahoma. His heritage stems from both Cherokee and Irish descent. He was born in poverty and was a shy introvert. Chuck's mother, Wilma Scarberry-Norris, raised her boys as a single mother after their father left the family following their divorce. Chuck was the oldest of three brothers and helped his mother raise the younger boys when they moved to California. Academically, Chuck struggled in school, as he was an average student. He was not interested in athletics either (this is something that many of us can relate to). After he graduated from high school, he enrolled in the United States Air Force. While in South Korea, he studied martial arts, Tang Soo Do, and later opened several karate schools. He began competing in karate tournaments, where he excelled to the top of his sport. This led to his accomplishment as an undefeated Professional World Full-Contact Middleweight Karate Champion. He has a black belt in Tang Soo Do and in Brazilian jiu-jitsu and judo. Successfully retiring from martial arts, his acting career began to take off. Norris is famous for his roles in widely known, popular action movies. Norris is now an actor, film producer, and screenwriter.

So, you ask how did God use him? Let's go back to his childhood. Norris' Christian mother raised him in faith, and as a youth, he decided to accept Jesus as his Lord. Like so many actors, Chuck lost sight of his faith. He strayed away, had an extramarital affair, and ended up divorcing his first wife. Realizing where his life was headed, he recommitted his life to God. The following article from GodTube describes Chuck's Christian walk:

> *Chuck recommitted himself to Christ while living with his second wife, Gina, and credits their relationship with resetting them on track spiritually, both as a couple and in their personal relationships with the Lord. Since that time, the Norris family has grown to welcome their twin daughters, Dakota and Danilee. His love*

for children led him, along with wife Gina, to create the Kickstart foundation, with the purpose of "building strong moral character in youth through martial arts training." Since its creation, Kickstart has been implemented in over 6,500 schools. Chuck says that, through his foundation, he has been able to encourage kids with positive affirmations and biblical principles.

"The martial arts is a philosophy that is pretty much the principles in the Bible. Even though we can't talk about Jesus, we can talk about what Jesus talks about in the Bible – love, loving your neighbor, being good people. Even though we can't quote Scripture, we can say what Jesus says in the Bible or what the Apostle Paul says, or what St. Peter says. We can say that in an indirect way, which we do."

In the entertainment industry, Chuck is known for his outspoken beliefs and refusal to back down

> *to Hollywood pressures. He has made a point to promote Christian films, most notably <u>Mel Gibson's</u>, The Passion of the Christ, and speaks openly about his faith on the talk show circuit, as well as in his writings for independent news site, WorldNetDaily.com.* [17]

Chuck is an example of second chances when we repent and ask God for forgiveness. I believe that God had His hand on Chuck's career even when he was not walking in obedience to the Word of God. God will wait for His children, but we must be careful not to go too far, as we do not know what tomorrow holds. Our lives are nothing more than a vapor (James 4:14). I like to remind people that eternity is a long time to live in torment, with no relief day after day. Salvation is a gift from God. Jesus has already paid the price for our salvation. Now is the time to accept Jesus as your Savior and Lord before it is too late.

> *Why, you do not even know what will happen tomorrow. What is your life? You are a mist that*

---

[17] https://www.godtube.com/news/chuck-norris-christian-faith-and-bio.html

> *appears for a little while and then vanishes.*
>
> *James 4:14 NIV*

• Corrie ten Boom

The story of Corrie ten Boom is an inspiring, uplifting, and an amazing testimony of unwavering faith. Corrie was an ordinary woman like you and me. Perhaps she was filled with doubt at times, as we are, yet she kept her eyes on God and trusted Him completely.

Cornelia Arnolda Johanna "Corrie" ten Boom, was born in Haarlem, Netherlands on April 15, 1892. She was the youngest in her family, living with her sisters Bestie and Nollie and her brother, Willem. Corrie was named after her mother. Raised in a Christian home, she was a Dutch Christian, watchmaker, and writer.

After her mother died and a romantic interest fell through, she trained to be a watchmaker. She was the first woman in Holland to be licensed as a watchmaker in 1922. Her vocation led her to start a teenage girl's youth club, offering classes in religion, the performing arts, sewing, and handicrafts.

During the Holocaust in World War II, the ten Boom's, Corrie, her Father Casper ten Boom (a jeweler and watchmaker), Corrie's sister Betsie, and other family members saved nearly 800 Jews from the Nazis. They were able to accomplish this by hiding Jews in her house, which was located above the watch shop, and other safe homes around the city. A ventilated, secret room was built in Corrie's bedroom like the size of a small wardrobe closet, hidden behind a false wall. This provided six people with standing opportunities only to hide. They had to be quiet at all times when the Gestapo raided the house. Corrie became a leader, overseeing a network of "safe homes" in the country.

During the war, a Dutch informant told the Nazis about the ten Booms, and the Gestapo raided their house. The entire ten Boom family was arrested. The good news is, even though the German soldiers searched the house, those hidden in the secret room were never found. The ten Booms were incarcerated, sent to concentration camps. Corrie's father and sister Betsie died while in the camp, but inexplicably, Corrie was released later on.

During their time in the German concentration camp, the barracks were infested with lice. The living conditions in the barracks were filthy and unbearable, where diseases were rampant. Yet, through it all, Corrie and Betsie continued to believe in God and knew there was a greater purpose. To stay positive, they kept their eyes on God during this extremely difficult circumstance. The sisters conducted Bible studies every night, and they even thanked God for the lice. Because of the lice, the guards did not enter the barracks, so the Bible studies went uninterrupted, and many prisoners were saved.

Once the war was over, Corrie returned to the Netherlands and set up a rehabilitation center for the survivors of the concentration camps, and because of her faith, she even included those that had helped the Germans in the camps.

Work after the war according to biography.com:

> In 1946, she began a worldwide ministry that took her to more than 60 countries. She received many tributes, including being knighted by the queen of the Netherlands. In 1971, she wrote a best-selling book of her experiences during World War II, entitled The Hiding Place. In 1975, the book was made into a movie starring Jeannette Clift as Corrie and Julie Harris as her sister Betsie.[18]

---

[18] https://www.biography.com/activist/corrie-ten-boom

Corrie suffered a stroke that left her paralyzed and unable to speak. She died on her 91st birthday in Placentia, California, on April 15, 1983.

Corrie ten Boom displayed a life of courage as she kept her eyes on God's mercy and grace amidst horrible circumstances. She trusted God with unwavering faith. Let's summarize what she did: she hid the Jews, she was incarcerated because of the good she did for the Jews, she was incarcerated in a building that was full of lice, people were dying all around her because of the treacherous conditions, yet she kept her eyes on God, and she even prayed for the lice. When Corrie was released from the concentration camp, she continued to help those incarcerated and those who helped the Germans. She began a worldwide ministry covering 60 countries. Her life was not easy, but she refused to think only of herself. Instead, she showed love towards others. Mark 12:30-31 reminds us that we are to love the Lord our God and to love our neighbor as ourselves. I would say, "Corrie went above and beyond the call of duty."

> *Love the Lord your God with all your heart and with all your soul and with all your mind and with all your strength.' The second is this: 'Love your neighbor as your-*

> *self.' There is no commandment greater than these."*
> *Mark 12:30-31 NIV*

Information taken from:
https://jimdaly.focusonthefamily.com/meet-two-ordinary-people-god-used-accomplish-great-things-2/

https://www.biography.com/activist/corrie-ten-boom

Chapter 9

Transformation

Life is a transformation, but as a Christian, what does this mean? Let's start with what the Bible reveals in 2 Corinthians 3:18:

> *And we all, who with unveiled faces contemplate the Lord's glory, are being transformed into his image with ever-increasing glory, which comes from the Lord, who is the Spirit.*
> *2 Corinthians 3:18 NIV*

In the <u>New Testament Recovery Version,</u> Note 7 on this verse explains that:

> *"When we with unveiled face are beholding and reflecting the glory of the Lord, He infuses us with the elements of what He is and what He has done. Thus, we are being*

Life's Journey

> *transformed metabolically to have His life shape by His life power with His life essence; that is, we are being transfigured, mainly by the renewing of our mind (Rom. 12:2), into His image.* Being transformed *indicates that we are in the process of transformation."*[19]

> *Do not conform to the pattern of this world, but be transformed by the renewing of your mind. Then you will be able to test and approve what God's will is —his good, pleasing and perfect will.*
> *Romans 12:2 NIV*

The Cambridge dictionary defines transformation as:

> A complete change in the appearance or character of something or someone, especially so that that thing or person is improved.[20]

---

[19] https://blog.biblesforamerica.org/what-is-transformation-in-the-bible/

[20] https://dictionary.cambridge.org/dictionary/english/transformation

Since we are born into a sinful nature, we need to understand what the Word of God instructs. Let's take a look at some steps we can follow to enhance our walk with the Lord by renewing our minds into His image.

- Romans 10:9-10 requires an oral declaration of our belief that Jesus is Lord. You may ask, what does that mean? This means that we acknowledge Jesus' divine sovereignty, we pledge our allegiance to Him, even when others try to pull us away to an allegedly better way of life, and we confess that Jesus Christ is the Son of God, the Second Person of the Trinity. To receive the gift of salvation, we need to speak with our mouth that Jesus is Lord and believe with our hearts that God raised Him from the dead. This means that we acknowledge that Jesus not only died on the cross, but He has risen and is seated at the right hand of the Father.

If you declare with your mouth, "Jesus is Lord," and believe in your heart that God raised him from the dead, you will be saved. For it is with your heart that you believe and are justified, and

it is with your mouth that you
profess your faith and are saved.
Romans 10:9-10 NIV

- We must set aside time to communicate with God that is read the Bible daily. The Word, or the Bible, is one way that God speaks to us. Don't just read the Bible, but take time to study it. Once this is done, apply what you have learned into your daily life. The Bible is filled with many scriptures enabling you to walk in the light of God, to be transformed to do the will of God, and live a blessed life, and be filled with the peace that only God can provide. You can listen to preachers or podcasts, but the best way to learn is to listen to what God has to say to you by reading the Bible.
- Prayer is another essential way to communicate with God. We are to start our day by praying to God with words of praise and thanksgiving for what He is doing and has done for us. This is honoring to Him. When we pray with words of praise and thanksgiving, we are saying that we love Him and grateful for all He does. We are to pray for the needs of the people around us and afar, for the sick, for those struggling with addictions, for those with

financial needs, family issues, and for whatever God puts on our hearts. Then you are to pray for your own needs. In everything, we are to thank God for giving us another day, for answers to prayers, and for His mercy, grace, and protection. God is always ready to hear from us, any time of the day, 24 hours a day, and seven days a week.

- Find a sound, Bible-teaching church. There are many churches that water down the message of God's Word to appease the current culture. The easiest way to feel connected in church is by getting involved with a ministry that holds your interest. Some ministries that you can be involved in include: choir, teaching, men's or women's ministries, missionary outreach, volunteering for the church's needs, and evangelism. Connecting with other believers can help us cope with life and be an encouragement during times of trials and tribulation. Hebrews 10:25 reminds us not to neglect assembling with one another.

Not giving up meeting together,
as some are in the habit of doing,
but encouraging one another.
Hebrews 10:25 NIV

Life's Journey

- In all circumstances, we are to be grateful, giving thanks for all the Lord is doing for us. When we feel God doesn't care, be assured that He is working behind the scenes. We need to practice patience, believing God knows all things and that He cares for us. The book of John, chapter 11, contains the story of Lazarus. Lazarus of Bethany was the brother of Mary and Martha, and all of them were close friends of Jesus. Yet, when Jesus heard that Lazarus was sick, he did not rush to heal him so that He would be able to demonstrate the glory of God. When Jesus arrived at Lazarus' house, He showed compassion, weeping for his friend. Lazarus was in the tomb for four days before Jesus commanded him in a loud voice to come out. Yes, Jesus raised Lazarus from the dead, another demonstration that He was the Son of God. He did this so that others would believe. Remember, God's timing is accurate. We must be patient, knowing that if He does not answer our prayers immediately, it is because He has a greater plan for good in His preferred timing.
- When we make mistakes or fail on our journey in this life, we shouldn't be too hard on ourselves, knowing that God

has compassion on us and that He cares for us. Repent, ask God for forgiveness, and go forward. Don't look back. In John 10:28-29, Jesus says that *"no one will snatch his children from His hand nor His Father's hand because He gives eternal life that will never perish."* Remember, Jesus is trustworthy. In 2 Timothy 2:11-13, it says, *"if we disown Him, he will also disown us but if we are faithful, He will be faithful."*

I give them eternal life, and they shall never perish; no one will snatch them out of my hand. My Father, who has given them to me, is greater than all; no one can snatch them out of my Father's hand.
John 10:28-29 NIV

Here is a trustworthy saying: If we died with him, we will also live with him; if we endure, we will also reign with him. If we disown him, he will also disown us; if we are faithless, he remains faithful, for he cannot disown himself.
2 Timothy 2:11-13

Chapter 10

Conclusion

As God uses people to accomplish His eternal goal, He also uses these same people to encourage others. He does not use perfect people, as no one would qualify. He uses the poor, often taking them from rags to riches. He uses the weak and even uses kings. The examples of Ruth, Queen Ester, Tyler Perry, and De Won Chang demonstrate that despite many struggles and challenges and by not giving up on their dreams or faith in God, His will for each of their lives was accomplished. God uses the weak because He knows that when we are weak, there is no doubt that our strength comes from Him, and we humbly accept the challenges of this life with gratitude.

God's grace doesn't stop there, and His loves extend to those that have been cheated by life's mishaps, like Mephibosheth. God redeemed Mephibosheth after he became crippled and lost everything when his father and grandfather died. God came through for him by using King David to restore his wealth (even the interest he would have received) and provide caregivers to help him in his compromised condition. Let's not forget Cornealious Anderson, a man that was given a second chance due to a clerical error. Because of this miraculous oversight, his life was dedicated to God as he pursued a life of helping and serving others.

Without a doubt, Jesus' life was met with horrific battles, yet He was obedient to His Father because of His love for humanity. Jesus waited patiently for God, knowing that God would never fail Him. Jesus demonstrated great patience while he hung on the cross, carrying our sins on His shoulders. God had to turn away from His only Son because of His love, knowing this was the only way for us to be saved. Salvation comes only through the acceptance of Jesus Christ as our messiah and savior.

So, let me leave you with these thoughts of encouragement:

- We all go through challenges that can last for a season or years.
- No matter how far we stray from God, God will set our feet back on the right path when we confess our sins and repent.

- God values the faith we have in Him, despite our shortcomings.
- We are to wait upon the Lord to accomplish our heart's desire and the plan He has for us. His timing is always perfect.
- He will never forsake us.
- He will carry us until the end.
- Do not forget, the main goal of this life is to spread the Gospel of Jesus Christ and keep our eyes on the kingdom of God so that when we take our last breath here on earth, we will wake up in heaven.

STAND FOR THE TRUTH, BE BRAVE, AND WAIT UPON THE LORD.

About the Author

The writer grew up with ten members in the family in Los Angeles, California, where she was born. Her son Ben and wife Angeleena and family live in Idaho.

Elena obtained a bachelor's degree from Cal State Fullerton in Business Administration Accounting.

She worked for over 40 years in the financial industry. As a Loan Officer, she approved and processed loans from small signature loans to corporate loans and anything in between. Her favorite type of loan was processing Real Estate Loans as she enjoyed in the excitement as people purchase their residence. She retired as the Mortgage Servicing Administrator.

She is the writer of "Turn to God from Idols" and "A Call from God."

Her love for God continues to grow as she studies and understands the magnitude of God's love for us, and she put her faith and trust in Him.